Paris, 1954 - Dori Jeanine browsing the bookstalls by
Notre Dame.

SERENITY

Positive Paths to Inner Peace

DORI JEANINE SOMERS

SERENITY
POSITIVE PATHS TO INNER PEACE

iUniverse books may be ordered through booksellers or by contacting:

iUniverse LLC
1663 Liberty Drive
Bloomington, IN 47403
www.iuniverse.com
1-800-Authors (1-800-288-4677)

Because of the dynamic nature of the Internet, any web addresses or links contained in this book may have changed since publication and may no longer be valid. The views expressed in this work are solely those of the author and do not necessarily reflect the views of the publisher, and the publisher hereby disclaims any responsibility for them.

ISBN: 978-1-4917-4356-0 (sc)
ISBN: 978-1-4917-4355-3 (e)

Library of Congress Control Number: 2014914776

Printed in the United States of America.

iUniverse rev. date: 08/23/2014

DEDICATION

for family—
those given by birth
those chosen in warmth and affection
and
for the children, grown—
once denizens of Dori's Dorm

CONTENTS

ILLUSTRATIONS

Joy City

Love Lake

Laughter Light

Creativity Creek

Beauty Bay

Responsible Mountain

Enthusiasm Park

Tranquility Pond

Forgiving Foothills

Respect River

Grow and Change Crossroads

Optimism Depot

Generous Junction

Mindfulness Meadow

Gratitude Farms

Kindness Corners

State of Serenity

N
W   E
S

This map. . .will serve to point the way, but the journey
is in the stories that follow.

PREFACE

The Journey Begins

Guidebook

We are not seeking sanctuary from the world
Nor rubrics for traversing life untouched,
Nor even perfect rules for righteousness...
But only this, a hiker's well-chose pack,
Survival tools, and friends to share the road,
That we may make life's journey
In the world, together and with love.

In the eighties, amid tales of burnout, bitterness and biofeedback, we were stress-monitored, stressed-out, and stress-related. Even our stonewashed jeans were stressed. The most popular of psychological buzzwords was "stress management." Aha! I thought, I'll write a book to share my peaceful techniques for living, and call it *Serenity Management* (quiet laughter). If we are to find our way to the calm within ourselves, I thought, it is not our stress we must manage, but our serenity.

Today I present the book, but today nobody would see the joke, so... in the spirit of Will Strunk and E. B. White's "little book", *Elements of Style*, I'll avoid unnecessary words to give you simply *Serenity*. Or at least a hand-drawn map to that lovely destination. It is my dream that this, too, might be a "little book" looked to for guidance in avoiding the crippling effects of negativity. At the publication of my last book, a friend sweetly accused me of being militantly positive. That apparent oxymoron charmed me into noting with my subtitle my intention to lead the reader on a journey to the positive.

What makes life meaningful? What enables us to find peace of mind? What gives us joy? These are questions we must answer in order to discover that cluster of techniques that brings serenity. Many of us are scattered in our thinking, chaotic in our planning, confused as to our destination, and short in memory. Some of us make rules and lists to soothe the mind and smooth the road. Thus we begin with a list of rules.

* Be Kind.
* Respect yourself and others.
* Be responsible.
* Forgive.
* Be grateful and giving.
* Expect the best.
* Grow and change.
* Be here now.
* Cultivate inner quiet.
* Be passionate, get excited!

* Honor and share beauty.
* Free your creativity.
* Laugh! Be outrageous.
* Love.
* Choose Joy.

This map, these exhortations, will serve to point the way, but the journey is in the stories that follow.

Extras

Focus * Get organized

These extras might be the cherry on top of a sundae. Or perhaps they're an appetizer coaxing you to take the first bite of a peaceable feast. Your guide on the journey to serenity suggests (firmly) that you begin this adventure with your heart and mind focused.

In the stories that follow there will be many names you don't recognize and people you will never know. Forgive me. My stories are always about people, sometimes quotable people, and as a writer I am obsessive about attribution. So if too often I seem to be name-dropping, and many are names unknown to you, I beg your indulgence.

In the original *Dori Jeanine's list*, getting organized comes first. First, not because it is most important, but because getting it done and off your *to do* reminders will free you for those things which you are likely to consider more important. If you have arranged your time and space, your musts and wants, duties and favors, your companion animals and reading lamps in an orderly fashion, you can begin to relax and free your thoughts to take you where you most desire to go. Soon you'll begin to recognize your inner resources, your gifts and talents. Now as you turn page after page, you can discover how to tap the gentle power within, and claim your own serenity.

Tune in your power.

. . .appreciates irony, winks at error, and has a big sense of humor

CHAPTER ONE

Kindness Corners

Be kind.

There is a word upon our lips as we begin our time together, a word to send us softly on our way—

The word is KINDNESS.

Mind it well and help to clear
The world of violence, of anguish, and of fear.

Kind words and acts and thoughts will not allow
For rudeness, exploitation, force or lies.
Kindness keeps us care-filled for the earth
And all her creatures, waters, plants and skies.

If all babes born and to be born were kind
They would find sharing is a path to joy
And giving brings delight; that each young mind
Can tap an inner beauty to employ.

The arts would flourish, peace would be our way,
And families would thrive and love would stay.

There's another old-fashioned word that has had some extremely bad press in America. Literary critics and English teachers hate it. And the public often uses it almost as an insult, looking down the nose. The word is *nice.* Can't you just hear the negativity when some people use that word? You can see it in the curl of the lip, the sneer, the superior brow. You can hear it in the whine of the voice. "That's nice." Or "Oh, he was nice enough." Or perhaps a sarcastic "Nice work, Charlie." To simply say someone looks nice is to damn with faint praise.

Shout it out, friends. Being nice is nice! Being nice, being kind, is attractive, and yes, maybe even sexy, but it may require a new paradigm of desirability before our culture recognizes that. We may need to reevaluate our ideas about what's attractive and exciting, and what is mean, contemptible or boring.

The Romance of Kindness

It is actually exciting and highly romantic to see two slightly imperfect time-worn people walking hand in hand, to watch as one eases the way for the other, to catch the spark in their eyes as they share some inside joke or secret awareness born of their long, and probably not-so-glamorous, shared history. A person is truly attractive when finding the funny side of a traffic jam, or shrugging off someone's rudeness with a philosophical comment on the pressures that may have caused the gaffe. A nice person, a mellow person is pleasant, even-tempered, unruffled, easy-going, non-judgmental. She appreciates irony, winks at error, and has a big sense of humor. He never screams and curses at you, slams doors and punches walls in rage, or carries a grudge. He's kind. And it is time to note the meanness, the contemptible quality and the downright boring nature of rudeness, manipulation, and spite. We're tired of it!

I offer here, for your heart and spirit, a new paradigm of desirability. This way of thinking will require that the object of your desires display these amazing behaviors: kindness, courtesy, good-natured acceptance, a sweet disposition, mellowness! This kind of interaction can be exciting and romantic in spite of everything you see on TV, read in novels, or remember from your more chaotic friends' life stories.

What you must realize is that chaos and excitement are not one and the same thing. Chaos stirs up the adrenaline and so does violence, but that's just the primitive, monkey brain reaction of fight or flight. Passion can be romantic, but passion is not violence, it is intensity and dedication. Violence is certainly not romantic. Meanness is the antithesis of love and glamour. Perpetrating damage on another— whether physical, emotional, spiritual, or material is destructive and totally unacceptable. Period.

Some years ago, Phillip Slater wrote a book titled *The Pursuit of Loneliness*. An intriguing concept that.

The title suggests that loneliness doesn't just happen, but that you must go in search of it; you must create it. We choose our lives—create them by the way we choose to perceive them. By initiating the concept of pursuing loneliness, Slater indicated that some of us actually go out and hunt for pain. In this case pain in the shape of loneliness.

The book dealt with the American tendency to consider romantic only that which we can never have. It indicated we want the larger than life image on the movie screen, the (Photoshopped) body beautiful in magazine ads, the married and unavailable neighbor across the hall. That we ignore the sweetness of the gentle reality that is our everyday experience. We may even ignore the mate who shares a history and a family with us, and the real folks whose beauty is of a different order. Perhaps they are a little less slender, less youthful or less dramatic than the icons of fashion, so we choose to see them as dull or boring.

Slater's concept made a deep impression on me, and when I was asked to edit my poetry into the collection called *Weeds? Or Wildflowers!* The idea showed up in the title poem. The poet, Ric Masten, who had originally asked to publish the poems, called me a romantic because of the immediate and positive nature of my imagery. And I wrote:

Weeds? Or wildflowers? Only you can say.
And each of us is ever free to choose
which it shall be that grows along our way.
You're a romantic, my friend said,

and I knew he was misjudging me.
No romantic am I—
wanting only what I cannot have,
and yearning for all that will not be.
Rather call me the Creative Realist,
taking life as it is,
and designing my own experience
as it can be....
and so I choose
...FLOWERS!

There are other ideas about what romance means. The American Heritage Electronic Dictionary and Thesaurus lists the words *utopian, idealistic, unrealistic, quixotic, starry-eyed,* and *visionary* as synonyms for romantic. In my lexicon, idealistic and visionary do not necessarily equate with unrealistic. Rather, I find those words to be descriptive of my creative realist. There is, however, an unrealistic side to the romantic young woman who chooses to get starry-eyed over a cad who ignores or mistreats her rather than the nice guy who treats her with courtesy, gentleness, respect and good humor.

Demanding drama

Why do we demand drama? Why would you prefer a chaotic, crisis-ridden life, rather than peace and politeness? I believe it is because of our national addiction to the dramatic. It's that damnable *make my day* syndrome! Shame on us. We are raised with images of dark, scowling heroes who are in truth anti-heroes, meeting crises with guns or fists. We are bombarded with images of violence, and told it is normal—art imitating life—just the way people are. We should know better. That's not the way people are. Humankind is not depraved and submerged in sin. People are holy gifts, created by a loving power, blessed with both free will and the gift of grace. *To sin* is, in its original meaning, to miss the mark. And if our mark, our ideal and standard of right living, is love and kindness, we must be constituted not as monsters, but as potential lovers.

Why are there people whose lives read like a dime novel, bursting from one crisis to the next, from one horror to another? I was discussing this recently with a young friend whose former classmate, Sally, is one of those chaos people. Sally plunges from one bad relationship to another, from one loss or tragedy to another, laments one self-declared defeat after another. Everyone accepts that this is just the way Sally is.

As we spoke of Sally, my friend said, "You know, if you were to view my life story a few years ago from the outside, you might think I was one of those people who goes from crisis to crisis, too. There was the shooting that left my brother unable to walk, the invasion of the house where we were staying by armed bandits who tied everyone up and robbed us. There was the threat of retaliation against us for giving legal testimony, a threat that forced us to move from our home. On the surface that surely sounds dramatic. But I never thought of myself, or of us, as tragic or dramatic figures. I saw only how fortunate we were. My beloved brother might have died, but he is well and strong today; nobody was physically harmed by the bandits, and the threat against us was eventually removed. As I see it, we were indeed blessed."

Do you see how this young woman has created her life? How she has chosen and claimed transcendent joy in the midst of strife? She is one of the fortunate people who understand how to accept the gifts of grace.

The gift of grace

Grace is another wonderful old-fashioned word, albeit one not quite so abused as the word nice. I have long thought of the gift of grace as our blessed capacity to see beauty, to register awe and gratitude, and to laugh at our own frail and fumbling human condition. A sense of humor is a gift of grace. And so is courtesy.

When you speak of someone as gracious, having grace, what do you think of? How do you see that person? What are the adjectives that go along with being gracious? A gracious person is courteous, welcoming, thoughtful—and most certainly kind, always, in all ways *kind*.

There is an anecdote about the Lunts, the famous well-honored royal couple of the theatre, Alfred Lunt and Lynne Fontaine. The Lunts were married, and they stayed married for many years, in spite of working in that notorious black hole of matrimony called show business. A magazine interviewer once asked them to share their secret of marital survival. "Courtesy," was the answer they gave, "common courtesy." Perhaps it might be more accurate to call it uncommon courtesy. The Lunts had discovered a rare and precious secret, *the romance of kindness*.

Prefer kindness.

Some years ago a writer brought me a manuscript for critique and editing. It was titled "a journal of four loves" and illustrated what I'm calling the romance of kindness. In this book, the protagonist or keeper of the journals writes of the four great love affairs in her life.

(Part one is called "I'll Never let anything hurt you, baby.") The first man she loves is the classic mover and shaker, a powerful captain of industry. He is, however, married to and totally dependent upon a deep, quiet, and capable woman who loves him unconditionally, and whom our journal writer comes to love like a sister. Here is Slater's *I want it because I can't have it* syndrome. My advice: Send him back home!

(Part two "I've learned so much from you") The second lover is a social worker who had lost his love through suicide some years before, leaving behind deeply troubled children and the widower with his self-esteem damaged beyond repair. He and his kids move into the writer's house and their problems and existential gloom eclipse the usual ambiance of charm and warmth she had created there. Here we have tragedy and drama, and violence to the spirit of the woman. My advice: Take back your peaceful home!

(Part three "I love you; I'm sorry.") The third man in the writer's life is a beautiful golden tiger of a man who brings music and mystery into her life; but he turns out to be an incurable addict. He shatters her serenity, calling at all hours of the night and day (collect, of course), pushing all her nurture buttons, lying and making her doubt herself in a textbook case of alcoholic crazy-making. Here we have pure passion corrupted by rudeness and emotional violence. My advice: Stop being manipulated and move on!

(Part four "You're the cutest, nicest person I know.") Finally the heroine finds a friend—one who had been a conscientious objector to the Viet Nam war, who is funny, pleasant, ordinary and a truly kind young man. He appreciates her mind and her looks, and supports her professionalism. He lets her know he finds her lovable, capable, and interesting, and that he loves her because she, too, is easy-going, pleasant, and kind. My advice: Go for it! It's the romance of kindness. And a happy ending.

Here's a story of a different color, texture, and fragrance, the tale of a failing monastery, in which the monks hear some words of wisdom spoken by an old rabbi. The monastery was located near a synagogue and through the years the prior had become fast friends with his neighbor, the rabbi. As the effectiveness and energy of the monastery weakened and the number of young men inspired and called to the brotherhood diminished, the prior became desperate for help. One day he asked his friend, the rabbi, for a word of advice about the dying religious order he headed. The wise teacher made this esoteric revelation to the monks and their prior—*"the Messiah is one of you."*

The monks had no idea if such a thing might be so; or if true, to which of them the revelation might point. They asked themselves questions...Could it be the prior? No, he is awfully cranky sometimes, but on the other hand, he is always wise in his judgments... Could it be Brother Herman? No, he ignores his brothers...but he's so kind to the animals... Or is it Brother Julian, who heals our every sickness and comforts us? Or could it be me? Oh, Father God, what if it were me!

What if the words of the rabbi were true, and the Messiah really was one of them? What if...? They, of course, chose to take no chances and began to treat one other with extraordinary respect and kindness—just in case. Each of them even treated himself with a beautiful and extraordinary kindness and respect. As a result of this graciousness, they created an atmosphere wherein kindness reigned and compassion blossomed, and they and their works flourished and prospered.

You too, may be an undiscovered Messiah tucked away in your day-to-day ordinary life. Take this idea to heart, and remind yourself to be always, in all ways, kind. Make violence a thing of the past, and help to usher in an era of universal kindness.

. . . to refresh your spirit, and heal your heart

Chapter Two

Respect River

Respect yourself and others.

SWEETNESS

In this world plagued with bitter realities
Life is enriched by the faces so sweet
The flavor of honey in words of affection
The smile of a friend or a stranger I meet.

You are so sweet, I have said to my puppy
Knowing his mission in life is to be
A living reminder of God's unconditional
Love—perfect, endless, for you and for me.

While the cynic calls saccharine all that is gentle
And laughs in his bitterness, thinking me weak
I can rejoice still and savor the sweetness
Remembering blessings bestowed on the meek.

You are called upon every day as a caring, kind, and
ethical person, to struggle toward an ideal expressed

in all the world's great religions and ethical systems—an ideal of respect for yourself and for others. You are charged with loving your neighbor as yourself, and translating that into the reality of everyday living. That means meeting each day with hope and determination, recognizing that love and truth always exceed your practice and knowledge, and yet accepting your existential frailty and human potential with faith in yourself and others, day by day.

Self-respect

Respect is always double-edged. To earn respect, you must give it, and to give respect to others, you must first feel worthy of respect yourself. Thus, self-acceptance is a source of strength. Accepting yourself is first a matter of being yourself. Authenticity brings with it security and serenity, and respecting yourself demands loving yourself. You are a basic miracle... and worthy of love.

Self-love practices self-care, has a wellness attitude, and cultivates a gift for relaxation which is something many of us dare not even aspire to.

Ann, a San Francisco attorney who, day after day, gave her best energies on behalf of those in need, modeled self-care for me. Ann loved the sea, and in the midst of her urban work, she scheduled into her busy life a visit to the beach at least every other month. Sharing her love of the sea, I found her wisdom worthy of imitation. Ann knew how to refresh her spirit, and heal her heart.

When living in Maine, our family had the use of a church-owned parsonage near the meetinghouse. In order to have a place of our own we bought a cottage hideaway on Beech Hill Pond and dubbed it the lake house. One of the quiet pastimes that refreshed my spirit at the lake house was putting together jigsaw puzzles. My husband and I were carrying more than a ten-hour weekly client load as pastoral counselors in addition to our other ministerial activities and studies, and I found the engagement of both mind and body in puzzle building to be truly restful. We set up our puzzle pieces on an old German indoor picnic table of carved black oak, and placed the table beneath a window. When we were not off swimming or sailing, or popping corn and enjoying it on the sofa by the fire, we worked our puzzles by the window, gazed into the pine forest and found serenity.

Nurturing and caring for my houseplants or the geraniums, herbs, and begonias in my little container garden is another of the ways I obtain the tender loving care I need for myself. It's that old truism, *givers gain* at work. By caring for the plants I give myself a gift of life and love, create tranquility, and nourish my spirit. In short, the plants take care of me. This is an exquisite and inexpensive kind of self-care.

Schedule for yourself a time to relax and refresh. Cuddle with your animal companion, re-read a favorite book, return to the activities you loved as a youngster—dancing, biking, softball, singing in a chorus, acting in a play. And take that word *play* seriously; play with children or with the animals, play for fun.

Not too surprisingly, self-respect and self care demand that you separate yourself from toxic situations and from toxic people. We sometimes believe that we must be available to everyone, regardless of the effects on our lives. Not so. As a giving, loving individual you may be easily manipulated, used and abused by those with different and darker motivations. When someone saps your positive energies, carries in gloom or chaos, and drags you down, the right thing to do, most respectful to yourself and to the toxic other, is to move on. You do not serve yourself or humanity by allowing destructive people in your life.

Choosing friends

A group of young girls in our Sunday school once requested a sermon about choosing friends, and I started out by sharing a silly tale I no longer remember, about a parrot raised in bad company. There can be some pretty life shaking and dangerous consequences for those of us who get in the habit of choosing bad company. But how sweet is the gift of a good-hearted friend!

Emerson said, "Happy is the house that shelters a friend" and "The ornament of a house is the friends that frequent it." So how do we choose our friends and companions? How do couples about to marry choose their mates?

As preparation for a wedding celebration, I have always asked each person to share with me (as they might share with a beloved aunt who had never met the chosen mate) those qualities most admired and treasured in the beloved. Some of the most frequently cited reasons to love one another are:

- We have shared values!

My dear one is:

- Kind and caring, loving
- Accepting and supportive (I can truly be myself)
- Confident and strong, intelligent
- Trusting and trustworthy
- Patient and understanding
- Has an inner beauty
- Brings out the best in me
- Has a great sense of humor - makes me laugh!

We're comfortable together.

The verb "to love" in Persian is "to have a friend." When we look at the qualities people getting married love about one another, we're examining what makes them friends.

There's a piece of country wisdom that says old friends are always best, unless you can catch a new one that's fit to make into an old one. Old friends are those that last as we grow older and wiser, through our hard times and even in the successful times. And this is a true test—a real friend rejoices in his friend's success. The beauty of one life makes the other life more beautiful, and a friend has no need for jealousy. A friend who will become an old friend is one who affirms you in your efforts to be the best person you can be.

How do you find the new friend that you're going to train to become an old friend? First you find someone worth having as a companion, someone it's good to hang out with. And how do you choose this new companion? I think it all goes back to the beginning of the list from my pre-wedding interviews—shared values! You admire the way she acts; she's kind, helpful, confident and strong, fun to be with. She has kind eyes and a warm smile. You like his attitude. You admire his courage and honesty. He's friendly and warm, accepting, approving, affirming, mellow and upbeat. Probably you have lots of common interests.

Say, "Hello, friend."
How few have merited from me this proud salute.
There is a sweet and pungent flavor to the words,
Born of my recognition of a kindred mind,
My secret awareness that here is one
Who will know me and be known,
One who will speak with me of soaring things
And leave the dull and the pedestrian behind.
Each of us is a creature quite apart, a unique spirit.
Yet there is a joy beyond all other joys
In that special oneness true friends know.
Hello, friend.

Respecting others

Respecting others means accepting them as they are. Everyone is entitled to be respected as an authentic and autonomous person. Withholding judgment and recognizing that I am not the arbiter of another's values and choices leaves me calm and untroubled— in short, serene. The double-edge of respect for another and for myself becomes a gift to both of us.

We are co-creators of our own reality in the very present moment. This puts the responsibility for your life squarely on your own shoulders, but it gives you an exquisite freedom too. We build our lives, our relationships and accomplishments on a foundation of our own choices, attitudes, and behaviors. What do you build into your life, for instance, if you insist on being right?

The dangers of being right

It has been said, "It is never more important to be careful of your actions than when you are sure you are right." If you are to respect and care for others, you'd better recognize the dangers of being *right*. A favorite dinner table story shines a spotlight on those dangers. This is definitely a story, not meant to be read, but to be acted out by a consummate storyteller. Imagine the following script presented by a favorite actor or comedian. It takes place during an executive's business trip by rail.

Ms. Gloria Brown, V.P. of Snarffle Interface Corporation, was heading to a conference, and chose to go by train. This particular train, you see, was famous for it's dining car, its chef, and his *coq au vin*. Ms. Brown eagerly entered the dining car as the train got under way, and of course she ordered the famous dish. But then disaster struck! The waiter came back to her table shame-faced and explained that the galley was without the needed *pinot noir* and certain exotic spices and herbs. The dish could not be made. He of course offered every other delicious possibility, but not the coq au vin!

Ms. Brown was irate. She demanded to see the chef, and proceeded to chew him up and down, parading her connections, her field of influence, her extreme displeasure. She gritted her teeth. "Do you know," she growled, "that I am a personal friend and colleague of the president of this railroad! I'll have your fanny fired!"

And just about then, the train came to a sudden screeching halt and the chef quickly fled. As Ms. Brown fumed and fussed, the car sat on a siding and waited. And waited. And waited. Eventually the train began to move.

Then, surprise! The waiter came dashing in to Ms. Brown and announced, "Ah, Madam, I bring good news! We will be happy indeed to serve you your coq au vin. As we waited at that siding a helicopter delivered to our chef all the missing ingredients for the dish. He has created a masterpiece just for you."

Brown frowned and leaped from her seat. "Oh, no, you don't!" she screamed. "I'd rather be mad!"

How often do we do that to ourselves? How often do we choose to be unhappy, upset, and angry, or clumsy, inadequate and failure-identified rather than allow our pre-conceived ideas about "the way it is" to be proven wrong? A friend of mine used to be in the motorcycle aftermarket, and he often used the illustration of being right by having the legal right of way at a crossroad. It doesn't matter that we're right if a Mack truck is barreling across the intersection as we insist on (legally) crossing. We'll be right, it's true, but we'll be dead right.

How important is it to be right? Is it worth creating failure because I *know* I'm never going to succeed? Is it worth destroying relationships because I *know* that women are manipulative and grasping or that men are dishonest and sneaky? And speaking of dishonest men—consider Diogenes who made a search for an honest man.

Diogenes was a cynic philosopher who lived in an earthen pot at the door of the Great Mother's temple. The *Cynics* were the dogs or watchdogs of the Goddess. They believed they were living in the *Eschaton*—the final days—when everyone was truly bad and getting worse, and the Goddess would destroy the world once there was not a single honest man left on the earth. The word *cynical* descended from the implication that, despite Diogenes's lifelong search, he never found that one honest man whose existence was preventing the destruction of the earth. Of course he didn't... he was convinced that people are no darn good. And Diogenes managed to be right in his belief, his assumptions that no such person could be found. He created a situation where he was constantly proven right.

A story is told of a wise and kindly farmer at work beside the county road not far from a small suburban town. An intense and determined fellow in a blue sedan stopped beside him and called out, "Hello, there. Can you tell me about that town over the rise? What's it like?"

"Well," the farmer said, "What was the town you're coming from like?"

"Miserable!" the man shouted. "Full of thieves and liars, businesses trying to steal your purse. Not a friendly face in the whole village."

"Well, you'll find this town about the same," said the farmer, and went back to his work.

Not long after that a family looking for a good place to live came along. They had piled into their comfy wood-paneled station wagon (remember those?) and toured the area for about an hour when they saw the farmer, and stopped to ask his help.

"Good morning," the father called out. "Could you tell us please, what you know about the town across the way?"

The farmer responded as he had done before, "What is the town like that you're coming from?"

"Oh, it's a fine place; full of kind and friendly people, good neighbors. Everyone is industrious and pleasant... a great place to live!"

"Well, you'll find this town about the same," said the farmer, and went back to his work

Creating your own reality

We create our reality by our assumptions, and the only way you can be in control of your assumptions rather than being controlled by them is to be open to the possibilities that would exist if you were to assume something different. You must be willing to give up the need to be right.

Another way to think of this is that we sometimes put more energy and value into predicting than into having peace of mind and joy! You will be just about as unhappy as you choose to be, if it is more important to you to be right. Don't foolishly choose predicting that you are going to be miserable in the next moment and finding pleasure in being right about that, rather than finding true serenity and peace in the present moment. Be careful not to short-circuit your psyche so that you confuse pleasure with pain.

If you are convinced that you are powerless, you will have a problem when you accomplish something useful. After all, only powerful people succeed at doing something worthwhile, and if you believe you're powerless, how do you go about being right? How do you demonstrate your lack of power and prove that it's someone else, not you, who is in charge? If you've already succeeded at something, I suppose you'll just have to call it luck (which of course will never last.)

Or how about this—you could admit to being wrong about being powerless, and claim your success. (What a concept!) Believe me, it is far more profitable to be successful than to be right! You needn't be a failure in order to be right. Don't tell the world, "I'd rather be mad."

Respect in four requests

As we observe the manner in which we can best treat one another with respect, we might take some guidance from a group of youngsters in a New England Sunday school class. When given opportunity to state their needs and desires to the adults in their church community, and to be heard, the youngsters set forth four wishes. They asked:

- To be listened to
- To be taken seriously
- To be told the truth
- To be trusted

In short they wanted to be respected. Not unreasonable demands for people of any age. I am particularly moved by their request to be told the truth. It is vital to recognize that you don't preserve their innocence, protect their vulnerability or teach them virtue by withholding truth; you only model dishonesty.

Adults who interact with children, whether as parents, teachers, neighbors or friends often bemoan a lack of respect across the generations. However:

- If the children are not given respect,
  they may have none to give to others.

- If there are no early expectations of
  respectful behavior and courtesy,
  the age of rebellion may begin at the age of two.

- Respect the child and demand kind,
  thoughtful and polite behavior in return.

Then watch them blossom!

We need a civility covenant.

I recall a tragic death nearly twenty years ago caused by that horror we read of daily still—bullying. A little boy died, drowned in the Rio Hondo River during a flooding storm because he walked home from school, too afraid to ride the bus where school bullies had been terrorizing him. On the school bus there had been no agreement, no covenant to behave in a civil manner toward one another, no attempt at being civilized.

The root word *civil* is defined primarily in terms of persons in relation to society or government, but I recall teachers and other adults when I was a child using the expression, "keep a civil tongue in your head." This other meaning of civil has to do with polite behavior. The word that brings me hope in recent popular usage is the word, *civility*—politeness, courtesy, a courteous act or utterance, respectful behavior. I am glad to read of a concern among us for civility.

Sometimes in marriage celebrations I have used the word civil in its meaning of both government connection and courtesy. I honor two important aspects of marriage—the civil and the spiritual. "When two people declare their commitment, and a new family takes form," I remind the couple, "it is a matter of importance to all of us. The community is made livable by the grace of individuals joined together in love and mutual respect. Thus it is the business of the state, the larger community, to recognize and honor the institution of marriage and the civility which it enhances."

Congress once proposed legislation forbidding uncivil behavior among the colleagues, and I fear it never passed, or if it did, proved useless. Not a very encouraging picture is it, when our national political leaders cannot "keep a civil tongue in their heads." When representatives and senators are so rude to one another that they have to propose a law requiring simple dignity. The truth is, however, try as we may, we can't legislate this sort of thing. It is useless to legislate integrity, kindness, humanity, or simple courtesy. You can't simply require people to behave intelligently. So how does a community achieve civility?

The covenant

Perhaps the way it might be done is by *covenant*: a compact, mutually agreed upon and faithfully lived. The word compact is from the Latin *compactum*: to agree together. That requires communication, and it requires civility. We must demand of one another a deep and abiding respect. Demand it! Without respect and dignity all communication breaks down. In order to relate peaceably, we must have a set of norms by which we relate—a covenant that needs articulation, negotiation, and confirmation.

We need to know the rules under which we agree to function and interact, a set of responsibilities agreed upon together, stated verbally, affirmed, and given life in the performance. Relationships of any size from marriages and friendships to households, tribes, and nations will benefit from this openness.

- Talk it over.
- Clarify your expectations and behaviors.
- Make your covenantal agreement.

In Judaism the centrality of the people's covenant with Yahweh is honored and celebrated in the beautiful Hebrew word *hesed* which means steadfast loyalty and love, and includes in its greater meanings respect, mutuality, commitment, trust and trustworthiness. You can adopt the spirit of *hesed* to reach beyond yourself, break out of your perceptual prison and touch others with compassion. You can champion civility as the mortar that holds a community together, and kindness as the antidote for abuse of power. Recommit and covenant once more to live together in the spirit of love, or at the very least, simple courtesy.

Disrespect and loathing

Jean Jacque Rousseau has been credited with writing: "It is impossible to live in peace with people one believes to be damned; it is imperative that they be either redeemed or tormented."

Note, please, the use of the word believe. It amazes me how well Rousseau expressed the beliefs of the religious extremists. This quotation is a description of the inquisition, or the Salem witch trials. It is a clear image of the rationale religious fundamentalists follow today in their condemnation of LGBT persons, their approval of murders at abortion clinics and their attitude toward those whom they deem unworthy. If I believe someone to be damned, I will then give myself permission to treat them damnably. And what is more, I'll want my belief in damnation to be incarnated before my very eyes. "Show me, God, how you torment these wicked sinners. Let me see them suffer!"

Sad to say, we humans find grim satisfaction in seeing someone get their just deserts. Think about it a minute. Call to mind any of your favorite action and adventure novels, murder mysteries, tales of the crypt. We want the baddies to get got! Perhaps that's not such a bad thing in storyland. I like to think these tales provide a kind of catharsis, an emotional release that can free us to be forgiving and humane in the real world. But it is cautionary, isn't it?

We are one.

A mutual respect expresses itself as brotherly and sisterly love. If we agree in brotherly love, as Hosea Ballou said, there is nothing that can divide us. Without it there is nothing that can unite us. We are one. Interconnected. Interdependent. Intertwined. Learn, therefore to live with an awareness of our oneness and to respect yourself and others.

...touch the fuzzy texture of a teddy bear

Chapter Three

Responsibility Mountain

Be responsible.

Destiny's Tiller

Mine is an open destiny,
based on my own deciding.
I'm not pre-set—computerized to someone else's course,
But free to sail a new tack as I choose it.
The thing is to rejoice with each fresh breeze
And thrill to the sailing on the open seas.
The winds and the tides are given,
I don't control them.
Sometimes I find myself becalmed, "in irons,"
Without the slightest whisper of a wind.
What matters is that my hand holds the tiller,
When gusts from new directions fill my sails.
While subject to events and circumstances,
I have yet the choice of how I'll be
And feel, and act in light
of what life brings me.
I can run with the wind or tack,

That's up to me.
So I'll dare high seas
and trade away safe harbors
For the challenge, the excitement and the zest
Of deciding. I'm not fearless, just intrepid,
And my own hand upon the tiller rests.

Your life story, and the way you tell it to yourself and to the world becomes, in fact, a map or blueprint, which you make actual in a self-fulfilling prophecy. Feelings of helplessness are like a poison you put into your body; they destroy your immune system so that you see yourself as helpless.

You may not want to hear that you are responsible for yourself. And yet you know that each of us is one hundred percent responsible for the living of our own lives. (Even as we recognize that this can be affected by chemical imbalances from illness flooding the body with internally generated toxicity.)

The positive response

If you think only of blame and fault you will see the word *responsible* in negative terms. And though you may want to point to a culprit, to lay blame on someone, it certainly will not be yourself. But relax, that is not what responsibility is about. Being responsible is *being able to respond*—having the glorious opportunity to enrich yourself and humankind by responding. If you so choose, you can respond with nobility, dignity, and humor to whatever scenario life puts before you.

Respond is the word, not react. The great heroes in times of catastrophe are the men and women called first responders. They don't react—with panic, anger, confusion or despair. They respond—with aid to those in need, help for the helpless, comfort for the lost and broken. It is response and responsibility we must strive for rather than mere reaction.

Do you believe you can make someone else happy? Can anyone other than you make you happy? No. Your state of mind is your own responsibility. Whether you experience peace or conflict depends on your choices. No one else can react for you. How do you choose to see people and situations?

All this is about taking responsibility for your own life. Those who look upon the world and see only enemies could learn something by listening closely to the little boy who asks his mother why the "idiots" only come out when Daddy drives. That youngster will discover as he becomes older and wiser that his father's anger says more about Daddy than it says about the ability or intellect of other drivers on the road. And doesn't our anger, fear, or resentment always say more about us than about others?

There are three ways in which you can be responsible for your own life.

- You can exercise your own initiative
  and do whatever must be done.
- You can delegate some of your initiative to another.

- You can give up your initiative totally to others, if you so choose.

It remains your decision, however, your responsibility. Each of us is ultimately in charge of our own life. As long as you believe somebody else is doing it to you or for you, you can't make your life different—you won't be effective.

Imprisoned by freedom

The chairman of the celebrations committee in one church I served had an inspired approach to the job. He passionately pursued the themes and speakers that would bring the church's values into focus in the real world. His name was Jim, and his goal was to help the people tune into their own deepest held beliefs, testing whether those beliefs indeed provide the needed foundations for living. One of the theories Chairman Jim voiced many times is that life has become complicated and difficult since the increase in our society of personal freedom. He believed life has actually become difficult *because of* the increase in freedom.

"It used to be quite simple," he said, "when everyone stayed in the town where they were born, followed in their parents' footsteps, voted their father's party, married and stayed married to the right kind of person at the right time and for the right reasons. Everyone did just what was expected of them." Or did they? This idyllic picture of life before freedom may not be totally accurate, but for the sake of exploration, let's suppose that's the way things really were.

Freedom is rarely cast as a villain in American lore, but free will means we can choose either good or evil. So how do we reconcile evil choices with a belief in the inherent worth and dignity of every person? What are the challenges wrought by the increase of freedom in individual lives? What do we make of this paradox Jim presented? Are we imprisoned by freedom?

When I decided to investigate Jim's theory and write about it, I had a typically busy small congregation ministerial week. My responsibilities included producing the newsletter, running off and folding orders of worship, preparing for a wedding scheduled Sunday afternoon, attending a district board meeting as a Trustee, preparing the liturgy and choosing music and readings, then getting that sermon manuscript finished.

On Sunday I managed to miss breakfast, mistake the date and time, misdirect the manuscript, and mislay the sermon. All at once I found myself in the pulpit with only my memory of the week's sermon preparation to guide me on a paper-free presentation of the morning's topic. It's the dream, the nightmare we all dread, standing in the pulpit "naked" (which is to say with no sermon).

I believe it is the responsibility of the clergy to act as role models for the congregation. And I confess to a special talent for modeling the human foibles, all too easily and too often screwing up. But I also have a gift for forgiving myself when I create a mess or a muddle, and for carrying forth with a smile. And so, I told the congregation, I will model that for you once again and plunge into the message of the morning without benefit of manuscript.

I was quite clearly imprisoned by my own freedom from the printed word. I had to take the plunge, and even celebrate that freedom. A few thoughts got left out, but I'd been immersed in my subject enough through the week to reach inside myself and share the most important parts. And the congregation— kind, accepting spirits, all—happily welcomed the effort.

Through the years whenever something like this has happened, when a scheduled guest speaker failed to appear for instance, I was called to take responsibility for (spiritually) feeding the congregation and serving up what I laughingly called "Sunday morning intellectual loaves and fishes." No one ever fainted from spiritual hunger.

The two faces of freedom

Have you ever participated in a *Blind Walk*? During the heyday of the human potential movement this was one of the exercises used to open new vistas of awareness in the participants. It is also used in team building workshops as a trust game. If you have done the walk, you might let yourself drift into a reverie of remembrance, or you can simply imagine this...

You are blindfolded, and being guided by a trusted colleague or associate. This person leads you to an open window to inhale the fresh air, crinkles paper by your ear, drips a few drops of water on your palm, invites you to touch the fuzzy texture of a teddy bear, gives you a taste of strawberry jam, a whiff of fresh bread, steadies you over the doorsill to walk on the grass in your bare feet. And all too soon it is time to switch roles. You then take your partner on an adventure of tactile and sensory experiences you have created, remembering always to protect and guide and lead into kindly pleasures. Ah…what delights you can present!

When you visualize that experience, what do you see? What do you feel? Isn't it exhilarating to be shepherded through those sensual delights? Isn't it freeing? Might this freedom persuade you to turn over your personal power to another—a guru, a master, a god or system which would take over all your decision making, all your responsibility? Might not religious fundamentalists feel just such a sense of exhilaration and freedom letting the church, the preacher, literal Bible verses or Jesus do it for them?

And then again—how does it feel when you guide and gift your partner? Isn't this, too, exhilarating and freeing? It is now up to you to find the wonderful experiences to share with your partner, up to you to guide, to protect, to pleasure. It is up to you to take responsibility. It is up to you to choose. So this is what we discover—freedom has two faces. There is freedom *with* responsibility and freedom *from* responsibility.

The freedom that we have named *independence* is freedom that demands responsibility, and this can be frightening. It may seem to trap or imprison you in a struggle to find your own answers to life's great questions. It seems that responsible personal freedom is far less simple than "shut up and sit down" obedience to someone else's authority. Blind obedience would give you freedom from responsibility. That's not independence but rather total dependence on outside authority. It provides a certain security, and may seem comfortable or even freeing at first, but it is in truth a trap and a prison.

When philosophers and psychologists speak of these two aspects of freedom, they classify the people embodying them as "inner directed" or "other directed." On our journey to serenity the only acceptable course is inner direction. Opt for the freedom that rests on responsibility. Never mortgage your rights to free will for a sugar daddy who will make your decisions for you.

Tellers of truth

To be responsible is to be a truth-teller, one of God's Fools. In medieval times fools or court jesters were often the keepers of truth, the only persons able to speak unpopular or unflattering realities to the powerful. The fool was the one person who could safely tell it like it was when the nobles and royals might not want to know the truth.

Sadly there are those who use a hurtful truth as a weapon to damage someone else's self-esteem or charge into battle against someone's beliefs, behaviors, or their very being. William Blake wrote: "A truth that's told with bad intent beats all the lies you can invent." There is an enormous difference between telling it like it is, and battering someone with your version of the truth!

Often we have seen seniors or persons in authority use their status, or picturesque people use their sweet image as license to bludgeon someone with their own negatives. When at wedding celebrations I hear, "Lady, you tell it like it is!" I am warmed and delighted, but I am always aware the telling must be done kindly. I choose to find the positives and to strive for gentle poetic forms and loving clarity even if I must sometimes picture harsh realities.

When we look at the challenge of speaking truth in love and kindness, we see also the alternative of making a lie. There are little white lies, of course; and there are blessed ambiguities—truths that may be hidden within themselves. My sister's husband in New Jersey was the town pediatrician for many years, and he had one such ambiguous compliment he used for the less than beautiful child. He would smile broadly and declare, "Now, there's a baby!"

When a lie seems called for, ask yourself if there is some other course of action you might take. Is silence perhaps an appropriate tool? Certainly it is not necessary to tell someone you hate his choice of ties, when you can just keep your opinion to yourself. On the other hand, in some circumstances silence can be dishonest, too. It can be a struggle to balance the dishonesty of silence against risk to a relationship.

Recognizing the disparity between a family member and their prospective mate of choice leaves a mother or brother in a dilemma of indecision—if I speak my fears will I drive a wedge between us? Is the lie of silence a better choice than igniting angry defenses? My advice is to ask someone less invested in the relationship if they might be willing to confront and discuss the problem of the poor choice of a mate.

People who pry or invade one's privacy with rude questions may deserve to be told outrageous and bald faced lies—something fanciful and amusing, of course!

It has been said that truth must be communicated to the crowds by contagion, echoing the thought that respect begets respect, and only by living with love and forgiveness does a child learn love and forgiveness. By living with truth people, communities, societies, and civilizations learn to understand truth. Maybe like love—truth is a verb.

To hear the truth

Henry David Thoreau said, "It takes two to speak the truth, one to speak and another to hear." Truth can sometimes be as much the responsibility of the hearer as of the speaker. There is for all of us the danger of hearing only what we want to hear, or perhaps what we fear hearing. Thus the way we listen is a great responsibility.

When Amy was quite young her teacher put this unfinished sentence before the class: "No child of mine will ever have to—*blank*. He anticipated responses ranging from "...go to bed before midnight" to "...eat cooked carrots." Amy's response was "...lie to me." No child of mine will ever have to lie to me—never have to!

Why does a child feel she has to lie to her parent? To protect herself from punishment or rejection, perhaps. And so the hearer may be responsible for the lie. Tell the child, "If you break my favorite vase, please tell me. I may weep a little, but I will not be angry with you." And then follow through with calm acceptance of her confessions. If she knows you accept and love her through all her mistakes and missteps, she can trust you with her truth knowing she is safe in your love.

Creating a healthy home

A poster found in a Massachusetts card shop carried this message:

Home is
  where you can be silent and still be heard...
  where you can ask and find out who you are...
  where people laugh with you about yourself...
  where sorrow is divided and joy multiplied...
  where we share, and love, and grow.

In a nurturing home we listen to one another and we are listened to. That's what I call talking *with*. We openly express our affection, our pain, our approval and disapproval. We respect each person and feel like persons in our own right—noticed, valued and loved, and clearly asked to notice, value and love others. Even our quiet times are the quiet of peace and mutuality, not of fear or coldness.

Nurturing families are flexible and accepting. Like Knights of the Round Table, we gather at the dinner table to share our lives and laughter, our individuality and our solidarity. It is in the sharing of meals around the table we nurture character, familial affection, and mental and emotional health. Families that regularly meet at the dinner table are better prepared to remain strong and caring, steadfast and honorable.

Welcome your responsibilities.

Here's a professional responsibility I've learned to confront over many years—being responsible for generating sermons. First, naming a sermon has a little of the flavor of Las Vegas about it. It's a gamble! The newsletter deadline is pressing, a general idea or topic may be resting in the preacher's cerebral filing cabinet. The season, a particular event or the temper of the times may seem to demand a particular subject. Then the reverend person gambles on being able to sermonize on the just right subject when the time comes. A catchy phrase comes to mind for a title (hopefully) and the sermon is announced in the newsletter some weeks before it is finally born.

Who knows what may actually be happening in the writer's head by the time he or she must put words to paper, pictures to a mind map, or fuel to the fires of creativity.

A delicious challenge, that! You, too, will encounter in your projects or your career new responsibilities, and you can meet them in terror or good-natured acceptance. Relax and call on your wit and humor to find the more comfortable path.

Commitment is in the results.

The responsible behavior called commitment is at the heart of courageous actions, at the heart of healthy relationships, healthy families, healthy communities, at the heart of something we call success. To what are you committed? The answer is always in the results. Everybody is committed to something. We're all totally and constantly committed to continue breathing, for instance—it's our commitment to life itself.

We commit ourselves to the accomplishment of wanted results, and to a course of action for producing them. Commitment is like pregnancy. It's not possible for a woman to be partially pregnant or intermittently pregnant with the same child. Each commitment must be one hundred percent, anything less is simply a good plan or possibly a broken promise.

For some of us commitment may seem a downright subversive word. If we have chosen a "no rules, no fences" mode of thought and behavior, we may think of ourselves as free spirits, too undisciplined to ever choose to be connected and tamed by commitment. Yet, as the poet St. Exupery says, "to be tamed means to establish ties... an act too often neglected." Commitment is self-limiting, because commitments only involve that which you can and will do. There is no such thing as being over-committed, only over-promised. It's true, commitment does limit freedom with responsibility, with caring, and with goals. But we thirst for those limitations, because they are also life support systems.

In my ministry I have married lots of couples who have already been living together, and I make no judgment about that. Some people wonder why a couple bothers with the ritual of marriage after cohabiting in a manner that makes it so easy to get *unmarried*. But celebration of the civil contract and sacred interpersonal commitment carries a heavy freight of emotional power. It says two people have chosen to be connected. They have made a commitment to care for one another, to cooperate in the creation of a shared life, and they have done so with a covenant—a compact of steadfast love and loyalty, mutually made and affirmed before the community which nurtures and shelters them.

We recognize that commitment diminishes freedom, yet it can only exist when we freely choose it. Commitment is therefore an expression of the very freedom it limits. The strong person, the person who accepts the challenge, dares to commit himself or herself—to an ideal, to shared goals with another person, to building community, or to a way of life. He or she chooses!

Is the person who guards his or her freedom too jealously to invest in commitment truly free? Paradoxically, not. It is only by limiting your freedom with commitment that you become free to grow, to relate, and to become what you can become. When you admire courage, nobility, humane ethics, family loyalties, education, and growth, you are seeing the results of commitment, the quality that makes the difference. Every result in your life is the evidence of a kept commitment. Take the responsible path; grow strong as you honor your wisely chosen commitments.

. . . two islands, separated by the sea, clearly apart.

CHAPTER FOUR

Forgiveness Foothills

Forgive.

Being Human. . .

mea culpa— for evil done.
forgive me, oh Spirit of Life,
for participating in that
which has caused pain to another.
mea culpa—for kindness left undone
forgive me, oh Spirit of Life,
for my true sin of inertia
and for my sins of shyness,
cowardice, and sloth..
Help me to move beyond all this
into my sacred center,
my essence
divine.

Now for the hard part, we must learn to forgive.

To forgive is to *give* up what has gone be*fore*—to let it go! And it's also being for (in favor of) giving a wonderful gift to yourself, the gift of reconciliation. Here are some of my favorite anonymous truths about forgiveness:

- *All forgiveness is a gift to yourself.*
- *You don't forgive to change the past;*
  you forgive to change the future.
- *To forgive is to set the prisoner free*
  and then discover the prisoner was you.

Add to those two with attribution:

- *Be kind to one another, tenderhearted, forgiving each*
  other

Ephesians 4:32

- *To err is human; to forgive divine. Alexander Pope*

Do not, like the person who would rather be mad than wrong, refuse to forgive and cling to your anger, allowing it to eat away at your inner peace and isolate you. As my friend Peggy would say, don't enshrine your resentment and build a parking lot around it. Don't drag around the corpse of a dead yesterday, missing the joys of today and tomorrow.

If you're paying attention, you will see that a *grudge* is a nasty, ugly, rabid creature with poisonous quills, and that carrying one around is extremely dangerous. To be unforgiving is toxic. Failing to forgive makes you a victim, stunts your growth and gives you an excuse for failing to live up to your potential. But be aware that a non-forgiver is not an innocent victim, but a volunteer. You needn't succumb to grudge holding even if it makes a good story. Holding a grudge (refusing to forgive) is a choice—a bad choice.

We all have our stories, and the tales of our perceived abuses and insults all too often become our self-sought identity. "My story is better than your story," we say, and tell our sad tale over and over again. But our emotions, behaviors, and peace of mind will change according to how we tell the tale.

The gift of forgiveness

I was once challenged to tell my story of a woman whose presence in my life had been accompanied by great loss and heartache. Some time after she left my presence, a U. S. agent interviewed me about Ms. Black while investigating her for a government position. I affirmed her national loyalty, non-addict status, and financial stability but refused to make any comment that could be tainted by memories of a broken heart. I assured the investigator that I was not able at that time to make unbiased comment on her character. I did not speak of it to the stranger in my study, but telling him only neutral facts without judgment affirmed for me the healing I had wrought for myself by choosing to forgo anger and blame.

Years later, after passage of the freedom of information act, Ms. Black sent me a copy of that interview with a note something like this:

I know you didn't do this "for me"
but I admire your grace under pressure,
and I salute your honorable behavior
in a difficult situation.

From a woman I was expected to despise I learned that I'd done the forgiving thing. I'd actually been living according to that which I affirm. Try it. You will find peace and joy in your authenticity.

As Ms. Black said, the forgiveness in that government report was not for her; forgiveness is not done to make another person feel better. It is for your own spiritual and emotional health. Think of the parent who disowns a son because he marries the wrong person; a grandparent who rejects a grandchild for her choice of career or religion. Think of the brothers whose foolish disagreement tears apart the very fabric of their familial love. Who is really hurting here? In truth it is the one who withholds forgiveness who is in the most pain. Oh, the one who is not forgiven may feel discomfort in the other person's presence or sorrow at the loss of a family connection. But the one who withholds forgiveness carries an ugly poisonous creature of his own making around with him always.

Story of the Buddhas

Imagine that everyone in your whole life is a Buddha, an enlightened being, teaching serenity. Everyone, that is, except you. But they all exist just for your benefit. The unpleasant, inconvenient or generally negative things someone contributes to your experience are designed to enlighten you, to make you conscious of a truth, a lesson you need to learn. The driver who cuts you off on the freeway may be teaching you to drive more consciously and carefully yourself. He may be inspiring your compassion as you fear for his safety and the safety of everyone he encounters. The person who speaks unkindly of you or thoughtlessly complicates your work or your leisure may show you a way to ease the path for someone else. So when you are *blessed* with really bad service at a restaurant, consider the waitperson may be a Buddha; look for the lesson; and smile!

Replace guilt with renewal.

Without forgiveness an endless cycle of resentment and retaliation eats away at life. The beautiful poetry of First Corinthians tells us *love* is not irritable or resentful, it does not keep count of evil done. In other words love, the supreme good, does not judge, blame, torment, or withhold forgiveness, even from one's self.

Forgiveness needs to be accepted, as well as given. Sometimes it is hardest to forgive yourself. If you don't open yourself to forgiveness; if you can't forgive yourself there will be no reconciliation. The culprit here is *guilt*. Replace guilt with renewal. Feelings of guilt are toxic, the poison of the soul.

Guilt combines self-hatred with anger, disappointment, fear of reprisal or abandonment, and hopelessness. When you have missed the mark, erred in your behavior, hurt another—you can replace negative guilt with a positive healing process of self-forgiveness. To aid you in remembering the process I've named the steps alliteratively, beginning each step with the letter "r."

- Review - Looking at your behavior honestly.
- Regret - Recognizing your mistaken behavior.
- Redirection - Changing your behavior. This is the major difference between guilt and renewal.
- Recompense - Paying what you owe to yourself or another—perhaps to both—a healing gesture, replacement of damaged goods, or an apology.
- Reconciliation - Making peace with the injured party and with yourself.

1979 - Alan was a kind and gentle man in his early sixties, with a giving heart, a bright and friendly spirit. But he harbored dark feelings toward himself, feelings of hatred and shame. Alan had been working in the entertainment industry during the fifties, and had been brought before the McCarthy committee and threatened with the loss of his career and what he deemed his family's very survival. In the hope of saving his family he named names and others suffered. How could this sweet man ever forgive himself?

As I watched the toxic effects of his self-blame and self-hatred I felt called to guide him toward much needed healing, and so I drew for him a word picture of the man he once was. I showed Alan his own story starring another young man. I spoke of the husband and father who had been forced to choose between economic disaster and ignoble faithlessness to friends and co-workers. This young man later turned his life in the direction of kindness and nobility. Then I reminded Alan that he is no longer that man, and asked if today he would forgive that other fellow. Thankfully, he did.

The forgiveness challenge

In various classes and workshops I've conducted with the act of forgiving among their goals nearly everyone has expressed a certain unwillingness to forgive. I must confess, forgiving has been one of the harder paths for me to follow in my own spiritual odyssey.

When I was a young businesswoman just starting out, I worked for a Philadelphia bank in a job that used none of my real skills or talents. After being at the bank about a year, I met an old acquaintance who published the Chamber of Commerce newssheet, which later became *Greater Philadelphia Magazine*. He knew my writing from previous works and offered me a position as a writer. My mother, bless her heart, insisted that I stay with the bank. After all, they had spent money to train me on an ancient bookkeeping machine. (And paid me slave wages for using one.)

In the spirit of her era, Mother insisted my first responsibility was to the paternalistic employer, not to myself. I was such a well-trained daughter, I obeyed my mother, abandoning my opportunity to perhaps become another Helen Gurly Browne in favor of Mom's old-time ethic.

In a wonderful open-ended book titled *Grandmother Remembers* I, now a grandmother, was invited to write memories of my life for my grandchildren. The book primed my thinking with questions like: "What do I wish I had done that I didn't?" and "What did I do that I regret?" I find that even the way I word the answers in my mind makes a difference in my being able to forgive or perhaps to forgo blame. I can say "I regret that my mother did this to me." Or I could say "I regret I hadn't yet developed the courage of my convictions." That kind of courage would have allowed me to assert myself gently. If I'd had the maturity to say, "I must do this; it is an opportunity that may never come again," things might have been much different.

Some years later, as the mother of four, married to a Universalist minister, I entered the denomination's Religious Educators Accreditation Program. In the process, I was inspired to take my education and my ministry further, and I made the decision to study for parish ministry. I had successfully completed all of the requirements for DRE accreditation, and went before the examining committee. Then I made a disastrous political error.

I joyfully admitted to the examiners that I intended to continue my studies to become a parish minister. In the light of this disclosure, Betty B., a champion of religious educators and member of the examining committee, demanded to know why I had come to be accredited as a Director of Religious Education. I believe I said something inane like, "I've completed the work and earned the accreditation." Betty was irate. I knew in my heart that the process had been an important part of my total education and my decision about entering a ministry, which I believed included the children, but I failed to make this clear. The group argued the point for several hours, but Betty prevailed, and they denied me accreditation. Not as they usually did this, with a proviso or the recommendation that the candidate complete the missing "X" and return for another interview. It was flat out—no accreditation!

The belief system I treasure tells me there is no one to blame. Betty B. was doing the best she could do in the circumstances. As a person of faith, she was protecting her sacred space from someone who held it in less awe than she. But when I look at years of genteel poverty exacerbated by the lack of that accreditation... When I recall the deprivations of my children, and the struggles for survival, it is not always easy to remember my principles of faith. I want to allow for the possibility that Betty was a Buddha in my life, sent to help me move toward enlightenment. But it has not been easy to accept without judgment her need to live what she believed—and she believed that I was not a "religious education person!"

A more light-hearted case of my struggle to forgive or forgo blame is all about my sideburns. My mirror tells me I look dreadful when the curl before my ears is nipped too short, and the impulse is to rant and rage at or about the beautician. Just think what power over our lives our barbers and hairdressers hold. But remember that even a terrible haircut will grow out eventually. So forgive, or even smile into the mirror and decide not to lay blame.

No againstness.

Peter and F. Roger McWilliams in their book *LIFE 101* gave my favorite definition of peace. *"Peace,* they said, *"is the cessation of againstness."* The McWilliams brothers teach that human beings are fundamentally good (or at least weighted slightly in favor of goodness.) They speak of looking into a baby's eyes and finding innocence there, rather than innate evil.

Looking into the eyes of a babe, we see purity, joy, brightness, and splendor, the marvelous inner goodness with which every child is born. If you reach down into that born-to-be-good center of yourself, you will reach a calmness and serenity that allows you to do good—not because you should, and not to avoid punishment; not because you are afraid or intimidated, but because good is the thing to do. From that radiant center you do the kind and loving thing as the natural response to the incredible gift of life. There is no againstness.

We carry within us a primordial knowledge of our deep connection to one another and to all that lives. Separateness is an illusion. I like to illustrate this with a drawing, but for you I will endeavor to make a picture with words. Imagine a sketch of two islands, separated by the sea, clearly apart. Come with me now as I draw the shore of each island as it descends into the water to become the bottom of the sea, and then, watch it connect! We are one. I cannot hurt you, my other self without damage to my own being. I remind you of this because it whispers a great truth about forgiveness. *Revenge is redundant!*

Like the McWilliams, I too have a baby story. I identify myself as a successful parent; I raised four children, and am blessed with nine grandchildren. My youngest daughter had the first grand, a boy, Justin Daniel. The second grandchild born was my son's daughter. My other daughter's son soon followed. It took only eight months for me to have three grandchildren and achieve what might have been instant matriarchy! As you might guess, I was often looking into the eyes of babies that year. I looked into the eyes of little Justin Daniel, and drowned in their pure blue depths. My story is about JD.

I invited my daughter Amy, JD's mother, to come to a spaghetti supper on the patio of my friend, Barbara, a great warm-hearted soul who made us welcome in her home for a variety of special events. Amy's husband Matt was studying long hours for his work at the Sheriff's Academy, so she came alone with the baby, who was sound asleep when they arrived. She carried his car seat out onto Barbara's patio. On the table there was a strange looking bottle with a small fan on the lid. Amy was intrigued by this mysterious object, and asked what it was.

Barb then regaled us with the story of outrageous costs the construction contractor wanted to charge for building a misting apparatus or cooler into her new patio. "It was just too much!" she said. But her friends had teased her and humorously feigned disappointment because she hadn't chosen to cool them with this expensive equipment. "So," she said, "When I saw this little misting bottle for sale, I bought it to cool my friends—like this." Spritz, spritz...

Some of the cool mist landed on the sleeping baby and startled him awake. His face crumpled into a wrinkly grimace and he shrieked, as only a six-month old singer can shriek. Barbara was horrified by what she believed she had done to the baby. "Oh, Justin, I'm so sorry," She said. "Will you forgive me?"

JD looked toward her voice and saw our Barbara's gentle smile, and immediately, a smile started in his eyes. Soon it covered his whole face and became a huge open-mouthed baby laugh. Barbara said, "Look at that, He's forgiven me." Sweet...

I thought about that charming episode while contemplating the idea of forgiveness, and it occurred to me that Justin had not forgiven Barbara at all. You see, he had never blamed her. Those heart-rending shrieks were an infant's response to being startled awake—a protest announcing to the cosmos that he did not appreciate such a rude awakening. But he had no need to forgive Barbara, because he had no need to blame her. What we interpreted as forgiveness was unconditional love. He simply saw love in her face, heard love in her voice, and unconditionally loved her in return. To withhold blame is an even greater blessing than to forgive.

It is impossible to receive the gifts of life in a clenched fist. If you hope to find serenity you must learn to forgive. We each need to develop within us an automatic *"forgivistat,"* an internal regulator of behavior that operates unbidden from our true belief that it is not our place to judge and blame. And as we mature and grow in love, perhaps we will even be able once again, like a newly-born child, to forgo blame.

. . . every time I write a check

CHAPTER FIVE

Gratitude Farm & Generosity Junction

Be grateful and giving.

We give thanks
> *For the laughter of the children*
> *Their love of one another, and of us.*

We give thanks
> *For each moment we are privileged to share*
> *Each smile, each laugh and tear…*
> *Each note or call or conversation.*

We give thanks
> *For simple pleasures, happy thoughts*
> *And joy so strong it lights our darkest days.*

We give thanks
> *For the kindness of friends and of strangers*
> > *for friends we've yet to meet*
> *For people more precious than things,*

We give thanks.
> > *And so it is.*

You should have no problem with giving thanks. It is not a matter of giving thanks to whom? Send out your awe and gratitude into the cosmos, the mystery of *The All, The One, the Holy.* Simply be... thankful. I have chosen to remind myself of my gratitude for material abundance every time I write a check, noting my gratefulness at the bottom and giving thanks even for my bills. I encourage you to do the same.

Make a little list.

Nothing is more peaceful and soothing to the mind than gratefulness. There is in fact a joyous celebratory effect to be had by filling your mind and heart with gratitude. I sometimes meet the challenge of chaotic freeway driving with the soothing effects of mentally listing my many delights, and recognizing my reasons to be thankful. I praise breathing and fingers and flowers, laughter and neighbors and trees, dogs and music and chocolate, the amusing 'glug' sound the water cooler makes that gives me a giggle, the blossoms on the dogwood trees...and so much more. Recognize your own thanks. It's powerful and refreshing!

We all need to express our appreciation and admiration. Allow yourself to rejoice in all life has to offer. Spiritual, psychological and practical exercises for years have included opportunities to list the abundant gifts for which, with time to contemplate them, participants are grateful. Silos of gratitude and abundance I designed for a spirituality class are simple drawings or columns labeled:

- People in my life
- My body and health
- Material abundance
- Creativity / Career.

Make your own. Label them like these or in any way you wish, and fill them up swiftly and joyfully. If you have never done this before, you may be surprised by the richness of your own life.

Every life matters.

Why do you suppose so many people call *It's A Wonderful Life* their favorite movie? Because of the deep truth hidden in that sweet, old-fashioned story. Because if any of us were to stop and consider fully the impact our lives make, we would be amazed. When the angel Clarence grants George Bailey a view of his hometown as it would have been had he never lived, we are all looking at the myriad ways our own actions have changed the world—touched the lives of others, brought new lives into the world, taught or led or influenced. You are important to the world and your life matters.

WILL IT MATTER THAT I WAS?

The girl was quick to smile, but will it matter
That her responses seem to light a room?
Her gift of sunlight made the day seem brighter,
Her laughing eyes dispelled the former gloom.
Our paths converge for what seems but a moment
Viewed in the vastness of the years between.

Can such a brief encounter make a difference?
Our lives are touched; what will it finally mean?
Each time another life meets mine, I wonder...
Each time I take the risk of being known
The question comes before me—Will it matter?
Will it matter when my son is grown
That he has been respected, loved and trusted?
That we each see the other as a friend?
That we have taken time for play and laughter,
And argument—with so few hours to spend!
It matters, I am sure—each moment matters...
Each life and each encounter on our way
Will change the world; and we will be immortal
Through all the lives that we have touched each day.

If you are caught up in the negatives of life, as a human creature with human physicality and the burden of outdated fight or flight mechanisms in your brain, you may not notice your own successes. Take time to note the goals you have achieved, the projects you have accomplished, the lessons you have learned and taught, and the growth you have experienced. We sometimes forget all that good stuff and focus on the bad. We tend to look back on our lives and remember what we didn't get, what we failed to do, what we refused to learn, and the growth for which we still wait.

Use a few minutes now to think of the things you have accomplished. Look at your life and notice over the past few years:

- Work and career accomplishments,
- Relationships and family nurture,

- Social and political goals met,
- Religious and spiritual growth.

What have you done since five years ago for your health, happiness and well-being? For other people? For your mind?

- What have you read?
- What in your life has changed?
- What habits have you forsaken or cultivated?
- What crises have you weathered?
- What new people have you met?

Have you perhaps smiled out your car window at a skinny, ill-clad young woman as she crossed the street at a traffic signal, and seen her respond with a surprised smile, and maybe a little wave?

We need to do more than defend our lives, here. We need to be grateful for them, and for the gift that is our very selves. Look at life's richness—its wealth of friends and family, films, books, plants and gardens, museums and libraries. It includes your own talent, ideas, and creativity, your loving, caring, wisdom, beauty, and thoughts.

Ah, thoughts! Have you ever realized what a treasure box you have, filled with your own thoughts? Sara Teasdale spoke of having no riches but her thoughts, yet that is wealth enough. The power of thought creates peace and happiness. It's not what happens to you that matters, nearly so much as how you choose to perceive it. Happiness depends on the quality of your thoughts.

Thank you, anyway.

Here's a story of gratitude I find particularly appealing. A young man was hurrying home from work and reached his bank's drive-up window just as the blinding sun caused the teller to draw the one-way curtain. As he sat waiting and looking at the blank glass before him, a motorized drawer slid out, and he hesitantly placed in it a check to be cashed. The drawer silently withdrew and a few moments later it returned carrying his money. He looked up at the blank window with amazement, and said, "I know there's nobody there, but I want to thank you anyway." Don't you feel like that sometimes? Don't you just want to say "Thank you," anyway!

Thank you, Life
for daughters and sons,
for golden light upon their path—
for Joy.
Thank you, Life
for those who care
to lend a hand when one's in need—
for Love
Thank you Life
for lawns and ferns,
for fans of green and wine-hued leaves—
for Beauty.
Thank you Life
for friends and guides,

for voices lifted in a song,
for Family
for Peace.

The other face of gratitude is generosity.

Being thankful also means giving back into the cosmos, having a gift for those you meet—even if it's something as inexpensive as a kind word, a caring thought, a touch. The wise ones of the world are givers. They know giving of themselves is priceless. They volunteer. They nurture themselves and others by giving of their time, their talents, and their treasure. Sometimes giving asks of you as little as a phone call. Sometimes giving is as easy as turning up the corners of your mouth and lighting your eyes with a smile. Dolly Parton, in the musical *Best Little Whorehouse*, said, "If you meet somebody without a smile, give 'em yours."

There is an epitaph on an English gravestone that reads: *What I kept I lost. What I spent I had. What I gave I have.* Let me tell you about Dr. Victor Olsa, who came to this country early in the 20th century from Hungary. He studied dentistry, eventually bought a farm in Putnam County New York, beautified it with loving plantings, made investments and grew prosperous. Feeling grateful for his good fortune and not wanting to keep all this for himself, in the nineteen twenties he gave the farm to Community Church, New York, for a summer camp, reserving the farmhouse for his wife and himself for as long as they lived.

Shortly after, the bottom fell out of the stock market and in what we know as the crash or the great depression, Dr. Olsa lost everything. The only thing he had left was the use of the old farmhouse he had given to Community Church. He told the church council, "All I have left is what I gave away." What a great truth! Each of us is mortal. And for each of us there is a last day when our life and its relationship to family, to friends, to community will be summarized in this one sentence: "All I have left is what I gave away."

Money is one of the most significant media through which we express our aspirations, our dreams, our beliefs, and our ideals. It is like language and other cultural expressions through which relationships are established, human needs met, values and purposes realized. We Americans don't talk about money. It's considered rude. Money is for many of us the last taboo. And yet there is deep spiritual significance in the ways we allocate our money. Money was an invention to replace old methods of bartering, a medium of exchange for service and tangible goods. We trade our resources—energy, time, and skills— for money. Essentially we are trading our *life force* for the money so that we can barter for what we need or want. Your priorities are made clear in your use of money, because money always goes where the heart resides.

Say it out loud.

Appreciation is a gift everyone owes and can give in abundance. But appreciation is incomplete until it is shared. It must be spoken. Say please and thank you; be generous with your praise and admiration. So often those who brighten our lives with kindnesses, with graciousness, or with their special brand of beauty are unaware of their own worth. You can remove another's self doubt, joylessness, and melancholy, even self-loathing with just a few words of honest praise. Beautiful! Delicious! Extraordinary!

The gift of accepting

Accepting compliments politely is an act of grace and beauty, the courteous and kindly thing to do. *Do not* discount a compliment! A discount cuts the value of that precious commentary. Belittling yourself or deprecating a compliment is insulting and hurtful to the giver. Notice how good you feel when you give a compliment. Toast yourself in the warm glow. The person who compliments you deserves that glow, as well. The fortunate chemistry of a compliment rewards and blesses both giver and receiver if it is accepted with a simple, "Thank you." Accept compliments graciously.

It may surprise you to realize that you give a wonderful gift when you accept another's gift or kindness graciously. Your acceptance of a gift is in effect acceptance and appreciation of the giver and it spreads joy. Gifts of grace are freely given and sweetly accepted—no strings attached. Gifts of grace are holy, generous, love-filled. I like to think that one supreme gift of grace is a sense of humor—the ability to fly like the angels because, like the angels, we manage to take ourselves lightly. Allowing someone to help you or to gift you with their time, talents or treasure is a way of honoring them and opening to them the joy of giving and doing good works.

Good deeds are admirable, of course…but when they are given with grace and tact they become truly splendid. A woman who understood the art of grace-filled giving comes to mind—she was an executive in a mid-sized corporation on her lunch hour. As she strode along the crowded street, she came upon a blind man standing at a busy corner, needing someone to help him cross through the traffic. She touched his arm and asked, *"May I go across with you?"* Now that's class!

We give thanks
> *for abundance, bounty and wealth made visible*
> *in the love-filled, smiling people in our lives.*
We give thanks
> *for songs and the sweet voices among us that lift*
them,
> *for stories old and new,*
> *and the weavers of tales who spin them.*
We give thanks
for memories that fill our hearts
and love that lives on even when we're apart.
We give thanks
> *For our hosts, whose grace, heart-room*

and hard work feeds us and makes us welcome.
And always, always — We give thanks for family,
    those given by birth
    those chosen in warmth and affection.
And so it is.

Give a few moments of your time, a bouquet of your regards; write a short cheery letter to a friend or a friend's mother. Everyone treasures a hand-written note. I am still smiling forty years later because the great Steven Fritchman gifted me with that special honor imparted by an occasional note in my mailbox. There is a law of inflow and outflow that teaches you can receive life's riches only when you make room for them by giving something away. Be thankful for the gifts of life. Give away some of whatever you have in abundance, share your "stuff" and make space in your life for new growth.

Epiphanies of mountains

Chapter Six

Optimism Depot

Expect the best.

Epiphanies of Mountains

Within my mind I know the mountains stand
And watch and guard the sunset and the trees.
Yet there is nothing that my eyes can see
Between forever and the darkening seas.

The air is thick and yellow, gray, or brown.
For days I see no sign of mountains blue;
Then clarity is mine one morning bright
My eyes are shown the truth I always knew.

Within my heart I know that God is here
And all of life is sacred, blessed, sweet;
Yet sometimes trouble seems to cloud my days,
To leave me feeling "less" or incomplete.

I wander on old paths of thought, and fear
Blinds truth, but then Love claims her own.

*I look into the eyes of a grandchild
And see the sacredness I've always known.*

*Each morning from the park I gaze with joy
Upon epiphanies of mountains there.
Whether pale and distant, or unseen,
Or crystal bright, I see God shining fair.*

*This metaphor, this gift shows me the love
That always is around me and a part
Of everything I do, and all I am.
"God is!" The mountains sing,
"Rejoice. Take heart!"*

Expectancy is living each day fully, keeping hope alive—
Expectancy has the power to sustain us—

The Rev Steven H. Fritchman was my hero, my mentor and my west coast father figure. At my 1973 ordination service in Fullerton he gave the "Charge to the minister." He challenged me to be "...a pioneer of a new age, a minister to the people, a woman, a friend, a prophet, a poet, a priest." He used the concept of prophecy, not as foretelling, but as telling forth, speaking my truth—the good news that needs to be spoken.

Later, my friend John Wyckoff urged me to trust my own strengths and to speak out the truth as I saw it. Especially when I referred to an authority and quoted the great minds he would ask, "What do *you* think?" In the fullest meaning of the word encourage, John encouraged me. He instilled in me the courage to speak positively of gentle strengths and great expectations—to share my positive truths with even those who much preferred angry negative attacks against all they perceived as evil.

Think of it as an adventure.

Some of us seem to expect to encounter the worst. Not consciously, perhaps, but that's what our anxiety implies. If you feel overwhelmed by your work, your volunteer projects, your hospitality duties, or your neighborhood connections, the most helpful discovery you can make is the one I share: *Anxiety cannot exist in the very present moment.* No more nail biting and awfulizing. Approach your job, your dinner party, or your community project as fun.

See your hosting duties, cooking and cocktail mixing as an entertainment. Play your favorite music. Ask for help; you'll be surprised how willingly folks help when you're clear about what you need. Limit yourself to making only what you know you can make easily and well. Know this—nobody wants to judge you, only to appreciate and love you.

Think of all of life as an adventure, and you as the hero. When the computer or printer breaks down, run to KINKO or FEDEX to rent time on one of theirs. Who knows what wonderful people you will meet along the way. Who knows what discoveries you will make, what treasures you will uncover.

When you can't sleep for worrying about that monstrous to-do list on your desk, get up and sing to yourself or chat with the dogs while doing a few chores and slimming down your "Chekhov Liszt." Then rest peacefully knowing your emotional and physical load will be that much lighter tomorrow. It's an adventure! And *adventure*, according to G. K. Chesterton, is inconvenience rightly considered. Problems can be the gift-wrapping for all kinds of blessings—like renewed strength, enlarged wisdom, professional-looking presentations, pleasant relaxed dinner parties, and new friends.

Of course the balance for that getting up at night stuff might just be to expect a little less of yourself. We all seem to demand too much of ourselves, trying to do too much. William F Buckley said, "My boat sleeps four comfortably, but five is three too many." Life is like that. If you can do four things in an hour happily, joyfully, productively, adding a fifth may make the list three too many. That extra burden will leave you harried, hurried, and distressed.

Awaken your knowing.

Shout your truths and let them fall as they may upon the hearts of those who care to listen. Authentic knowing of your truths is not simple knowledge, information, or collected facts, but the wisdom that lights your way from within. Here's what I mean when I talk about awakening your knowing. It's the "aha!" that sends a frisson of recognition through you, a "Well, of course" spoken by the mind when you meet up with your own truth. Emerson said: "Trust thyself; every heart vibrates to that iron string... Insist on yourself; never imitate...That which each can do best none but Life can teach us."

How does life teach us? Each of us discovers our truths, remembers them, or becomes aware of them in our own way. For some a movie or story echoes with familiar messages; for some truths become visible in our own creative works or in the artistic gifts of others, in the stories and traditions of our own lives or that of others. Do you ignore other people's tales and favorite practices and even sometimes disparage them, or do you listen for the life-enhancing possibilities behind the words and rituals, perhaps adapting another's truths to your own needs and understanding.

You might discover your knowing in a relationship— through a friend or family member's example, feedback or conversation.

For Hidden Gifts...
Every prayer a thanksgiving,
Every poem a prayer,
In burdens, quiet blessings,
In darkness, love and care.

Each shadow brings new insight
New gentleness or friends.
Each crisis brings a hidden gift
And sacred Joy transcends.

Every prayer a thanksgiving,
Every poem a prayer,
As kindness grows within the heart
And beauty blossoms there.

My dearest friend had one of those hidden gifts in the form of some really unpleasant happenings in her life—lost job, damaged career, multiple moves that required divesting herself of most of her meager possessions, and finally a promising new job that lost its promise when her supervisor was too rigid, impatient, and unkind to help her to learn the new procedures. So what was the gift? She chose to see this experience as a life lesson about how she treats her brother, and she had her own moral and spiritual awakening, moved on and rebuilt her life into something beautiful.

If you have any friends who are at all mystical about their spiritual life, you will sometimes hear them speak of life's lessons. It often seems that we receive lessons just as we are ready for them. Perhaps a clearer way to say this is that we recognize the wisdoms we carry within us, not just when they manifest themselves to us, but when we open ourselves to our own knowing. My muses put it this way:

OVERSOUL
Listen poet. Listen even as you sing...
To the music of a hundred million lives
Whereof you write unknowingly, somehow.
This life of mine, this self—this unique self
Encompasses the vast humanity

Of centuries beyond and yet to be.
A universal "knowing" sings the songs
In melodies that ring, reverberate
In every ear....familiar, although new.
I learn from my own saying forth
The truth I knew, but didn't know I knew
Until I gave it form upon a page.
And even then, the saying of a truth
That sounds so beautiful, so wise and good,
May not awake my knowing 'til the time
When life illumines words and makes them shine
In common things, in ordinary scenes
Day after day....as when I realized
That words my pen had scratched repeatedly
Were true...are true....That joy is not a thing
To measure out in moments, years, or days,
But in its wonders, and the "mattering"
Of lives enhanced, enriched, and beautified.

....and even then the whole picture may elude me until that time when everything comes together to make it clear in my everyday ordinary, extraordinary experience. That's what happened for a member of our church in Bangor, Maine, some years ago. She'd been in counseling with me for at least a year, and I'd been doing that curious tightrope walking kind of thing ministers and therapists are taught to do—asking the right questions, opening up options, teaching communication techniques—and all without advising, or directing, just encouraging the person to live up to her potential and solve her own problems.

In the process, there are some important principals that must be taught, but teaching doesn't really happen until its other half occurs—the learning. In the wisdom of the great Kahlil Gibran, we're told that learning will happen only when the student is willing to "enter the portals of his own knowing."

Then one Sunday morning it happened. Alice, the woman in this little story, came to me during the coffee hour quite excited, and declared that the needed insight had come to her during the service. The music, the readings, the rituals—the sermon— had all suddenly jelled for her, and she made her *discovery*. "That's what you've been telling me for the past year, isn't it?" she asked. Yes, Alice. It is!

Aha! moments

Knowing or awareness might be reached by meditating, or for some it's a matter of working in a Zen mode, nurturing your garden, cooking a meal, cleaning a closet. You might suddenly become aware, see a new truth triggered by a poster or greeting card, a children's book or one of your own more grownup books, novels, poetry, how-to or biography. I am particularly partial to poetry as a path to new insights, as you may suspect.

The exciting thing is that as you hear or read a poem you might discover within it something even the poet has yet to recognize. This happened to me as the poet, on a trip to Mexico to officiate at a wedding. The groom's brother and best man was my gracious chauffer, and we were talking about the inspiration of the empty page for a writer. I told him the story of unexpectedly filling an empty page in my last book with the poem "The Sea Is Always With Me." I had been grieving because economic necessity had forced me to leave my much-loved beach cottage, but the poem took me in a new direction and offered an awareness about that particular loss.

The sea is always with me. . .
salt of my tears,
the surging of my blood,
the dancing of my poems,
the music of my silent meditations.
Change calls me from these shores
and I could sigh and mourn
to leave the waves behind.
But oceans are not easily lost
and crashing surf
empowers from within.
I will not grieve.
The sea is always with me.

My new friend pointed out the wider implication and meaning he found in the poem. "This is true of other losses," he said, "and of all we truly love. We can mourn our loss forever or we can look into our hearts and say, That which I love is always with me."

We can open ourselves to making discoveries, to having a peak experience or an eye-opener. We can invite an *epiphany* into our lives. The definition of epiphany is a sudden intuitive perception of or insight into the reality or essential meaning of something, usually initiated by some simple, homey or commonplace experience. It's from the Greek *epiphaneia:* a happening in which the gods revealed divine secrets to humans. I have always thought of it as encountering the Sacred.

Discover yourself.

My method of reaching the *knowing* of which I am capable is to write, to compose, or to map my mind (Mind maps are drawings that serve as outlines and guides for speakers in lieu of a manuscript.) This kind of understanding named itself in the poem, "Oversoul" as the truth I knew, but didn't know I knew. Here is a gift I hope this little book might bring to you—a new awareness of something precious and beautiful you have known in your heart, even when your conscious mind hadn't yet noticed it.

Avoid doom and gloom! When the word "doom" flashed across my desktop I knew I had to inveigh against catastrophic messages. They come in abundance over the news, the internet, social media, and in the mail. Even the finest and most worthy causes may have succumbed to using scare tactics in their communications. Turn them off. If all you read day after day is panic-laden pleas for money, your time is better spent among those who report good news. Sad to say this warning may even include your church. If so it is up to you to change the messages your church sends.

Make peace.

When you are about to pour out your complaints unfiltered, stop. Think twice. Think three times, four times or more times, but think! Embrace silence even ever so briefly. Before you speak angrily or disparagingly, before you complain or criticize—press your lips together and think. Is it worth hurt feelings, scowls and silence to speak your mind? It may be. It may, in fact be absolutely necessary to clear the air, but first consider... is there a kinder way to communicate your concerns? What are the consequences, the alternatives, the beautiful possibilities?

Don't let bruised feelings fester. Find a way to gently explore together the source of a misunderstanding. Take possession of your emotions. Own your feelings and share them, but be careful—don't lay blame for them. Only you are responsible for your feelings. Say "I feel hurt, uncomfortable, grouchy when..." Not, "You make me..."

No one is without a religion, a faith, or philosophy—that set of values and ethics, understandings and beliefs about the nature of life, of humanness, and of the cosmos which guides behavior and spawns human emotions. Those who believe in chaos, cause chaos and live with confusion and anxiety. Those who believe in a rigid, authoritarian hierarchy, support paternalistic tyrannies and live with guilt and fear. Those who believe in themselves and one another create harmony and work for peace in the spirit of love. Those who believe in life's infinite possibilities—by living as if those possibilities were truly alive—awaken joy and hope and spread enlightenment.

Living as if...

Living as if—I'd thought of that as particularly my own quotable phrase. It was, after all, the center-post of one of my well studied belief structures, a way of creating the world in a better image.

This even as I, rationalist that I remain, recognized the inevitable unreality inherent in any belief or myth system, even my own. I know that my brothers and sisters on this planet can be cruel, stupid, even unutterably evil. I recognize the horror which is as much a part of the natural world as its glory and wonder; but I choose to recognize this, honor it, and let go of it, then go on to live as if...

...As if my dream of human dignity, brotherhood and sisterhood, humane behavior and love had indeed come true. As if the world were sane and safe and kind. The technique can be a vital force in moving it toward this ideal.

I heard another speaker use my phrase, and it occurred to me that it is possible to use it quite differently. I suddenly realized that everyone lives as if. The thing that makes all the difference is that unfinished part of the statement. As if——— *what?*

Those who live as if the world were cruel and ugly make themselves and their world cruel and ugly. Those who live as if they were helpless victims become helpless victims. But I have seen a man who was beaten, robbed, shot, and left for dead—so that he will be forever paralyzed—live as if there is beauty and love and kindness in the world, and so there **is** kindness, beauty and love in his world. He creates it.

It is only by living as if life were abundant that you find life's richness, only by living as if assured of your own success that you become successful. It is only by living as if life were a gift beyond measure that you learn to celebrate it and find joy.

The reluctant messiah in Richard Bach's little book, *Illusions*, tells us "...if you want freedom and joy...it's not anywhere outside of you...Say you have it and you have it! Act as if it's yours, and it is!" And Bach also says, "Argue for your limitations, and they're yours!"

You create your life by what you believe about living, by what you believe about yourself and others. You can change the world, but only if you change your understandings of what is and what can be. So you had better look to your *as if's*, expect the best and help to make it come to pass.

Vulnerable and flawed...
Forever the broken, oh-so-human self...
I live my varied days
Ordering my private chaos,

Patching my shattered moments,
my battered hours—
With humor, love, and joy,
With laughter, hope and creativity.
From what source have I
This mystic mortar of renewing power,
This psychic energy,
This always new and unexpected
Gift of Divine Grace—
'tis God's Re-creation!

When the Rev. Mary Murray Sheldon, senior minister of the Huntington Beach Church of Religious Science, succumbed to a serious back injury she moved north to Sebastopol and Peggy Price, her associate, was called to become senior minister. Peggy had just completed her training as a CRS minister and was totally new to full time ministry, yet she did a brilliant job in this extremely challenging position. A friend commented, "Peggy didn't know the task she had undertaken couldn't be done, so she just went ahead and did it." Don't we all sometimes find ourselves called to do the same? As George Bernard Shaw said, "People who say it cannot be done should not interrupt those who are doing it."

Choice is a holy word.

During the later part of my parish ministry, I had in my study, five blue notebooks which I'd decorated with lovely pictures on the front and topical titles across their spines. These became the home of the many clippings, prayers, poems, and quotable readings I'd collected throughout my ministry. At first I kept my clippings in a manila folder, which they quickly outgrew. Then several folders bulged with my treasures. At last succumbing to an attack of rampant tidiness, I decided to organize all that creative thinking.

I spread the multi-colored papers out on the floor and played a kind of modified game of Twister, as I separated them into categories or topics. I gathered related subjects into kindred collections and placed them in their piles and from there into the blue three-ring binders. I named the books Aspirations, Affirmations, Relationships and Creativity. The home of my deepest truths I titled Choice.

Choosing is among the most sacred acts of our lives. It is in our choices, minute-by-minute, day-by-day, that we create reality as we know it.

Looking through that Choice book of mine I found a quote written in 1900 by a certain Aunt Jane from Kentucky. It said:

> *How much piecing a quilt is like living a life...*
> *Life sends us the pieces, but we can cut them out*
> *and put them together pretty much to suit ourselves—*
> *and there's a heap more in the cutting and sewing*
> *than there is in the calico.*

Aunt Jane was telling us it is our choices that make our lives what they are. It's the cutting and sewing, the way we use what the cosmos has provided, that makes all the difference.

Making a difference

A thought-provoking piece of cinema I encountered many years ago was titled *Grand Canyon*. The events of the film take place in Los Angeles, and the oddly assorted cast of characters is both engaging and believable. These are not great heroes nor are they despicable villains, but just regular folks like the rest of us, making their personal choices in the best spirit they can, and thereby creating minor miracles and small epiphanies in a world much in need of love.

Simon, an African American tow-truck mechanic, acts as guardian angel, negotiator, and diplomat in a terrifying episode of near gang violence. He saves Mack, a white suburban attorney, from the tender mercies of a carload of South Central hoods. Later, in a conversation with Mack, Simon talks about his feelings of insignificance as he sat at the edge of the Grand Canyon some years before. "We're like fleas on the tail of a cow munchin' grass by the side of the freeway," he says. He likens himself and us to fleas! But the film goes on to teach a very different lesson— that we're not insignificant fleas and we do make a difference. We get to choose which side of the scale for good or evil will feel what Bruno Overstreet has called "the stubborn ounces of our weight!"

Sadly, the character with the most ounces, the most clout, the tallest soapbox or the best opportunity to opt for the right, is a filmmaker who features violence—blood and guts horrors—in his films. The producer has a moment of insight and renewal after being shot at close range by a mugger who is after his Rolex watch. He vows to give up his glorification of violence and make a different kind of pictures.

But then he rejects his own special epiphany, and denies the decision he'd made. He chooses to return to his shoot-em-up flicks, and he calls it art. A sad choice, made by a sad character—one who, by the way, suffers from terminal motor-mouth. He talks endlessly—theories, pseudo psychology and philosophy—he intellectualizes rather than living out and acting upon valuable choices. It's a malady self-styled intellectuals are prone to, talking and objectifying rather than feeling and doing.

I felt warmed and encouraged by this film, in spite of the things like homelessness, drive-by shootings, and street gangs, which figured in the story. I was touched by the little choices individuals made— choosing to love, to give, to turn to another human being in genuine caring and openness. Choice is a holy word, and it matters how you choose to be in the world because each of us do indeed make a difference to more than just ourselves. Make your choices with an eye to a positive tomorrow; expect the best and then help to create it.

...in a 12-foot Sunflower sailboat

Chapter Seven

Growth & Change Crossroads

Grow and change.

In Celebration of Life's New Beginnings
first published 1975

There is this to be said for life—
It's full of surprises.
The greatest of all is tomorrow.
It always dawns upon a world not quite ready for it,
And it comes in loaded with joy—
And pain, and bandaged knees
On little girls who've tumbled off their swings.
Some tomorrows carry love and friends and good news
Along with their cargo of dentist bills and petty failures;
And we learn that we can try and fail and try again
Learning by failing,
Growing and succeeding—sometime.

We own tomorrow, you and I
The freight it carries doesn't count
On the final invoice.

What matters is how we use it—
What of us we put into it—
How we choose to live.
As for me
Let me celebrate life,
The high moments and the hollow.
Let me sing life,
And quietly inhale its fragrance
In morning meditations.
Let me share life,
Express it, enhance it in human companionship.
Let me grow in it, learn through it, give of it. . .
Let me Become.

Chaos is the disguise life's changes
wear as they move toward order.

Picture the jumble of cartons and untidy household items piled in the middle of the floor as you prepare to move. Think of the clothes piled on the closet floor as the weather moves from snow to swelter. Now, write this down and tape it to your mirror, it is a Dori Jeanine quote to unexpectedly comfort you: *"Perfect order and divine balance and harmony give the appearance of chaos when in the process of change."*

Change is paradoxically the one constant in life, and you are granted the opportunity to grow and change every day. For most of us, however, change is stressful and unwelcome, threatening or depressing. Still you can make use of this process of change. Every day is a new beginning, and beginning now, in the now, you can start creating yourself as you aspire to be.

Beginnings, endings, and hope amid crisis

Time is strange and mysterious—a thing unreal. The time of clocks and calendars is something we invent. And so are beginnings and endings. We can look at events, at changes and at specific times, and choose to see them as the end of something, or as a beginning. In our culture we call January first the beginning of a new year. Janus, the namesake of January, faces in two directions, one face looking forward and the other looking back. And so it is for most of us in January at the opening of a newly numbered year— we look ahead with hope and resolution (s) and if we choose, we can look back with thankful hearts and increased understanding.

According to many motivational gurus, the word for *crisis* in Chinese pictographs is made up of two symbols: one for danger, the other for opportunity. Back in the sixties the term *Identity Crisis* came into our lexicon from the work of psychologist Eric Ericson. The crisis occurred when your self-image, your idea of who and what you are, differed from the image held or projected by society, or by the significant others in your life—especially your friends and family or those you saw as persons of authority.

The experts said an identity crisis happened to almost everyone at about 18 years of age, and maybe a second time at 35 or 40. But that's all, twice at the most. In today's world, with the constant changes in family structure, geography, economy, and culture it's a rare bird who ages calmly and sweetly, without many an identity crisis. But the wisdom of the East seems to indicate that even an identity crisis needn't be all bad—its dangers redirected, perhaps, by opportunity.

A good friend and colleague often reminded me that every problem carries within it the seeds of opportunity. This didn't, however, keep me from feeling a bit of terror over various more or less dramatic and unnerving episodes in my own life. Looking back on the newsletters I wrote in the eighties I am horrified by the heartbreak I read, the stress and the penniless panic, the feelings of aloneness. Happily, I had forgotten what it was like then as a single mother simply surviving.

Opportunity

After you've weathered some storm, look back and note: "Whenever the cosmos (circumstances) pulls the solid earth from beneath my feet, I am simply forced to scramble to higher ground." Things do improve. During the crises, however, it's hard work to maintain a mellow outlook and find the opportunity that's supposed to come with the danger. That hard work is what communicates itself in the columns of my old newsletters. The exciting thing is that emotions become joy as you honor your fear, and move beyond it to get happy about the possibilities. Celebrate *the divine perhaps!*

We enter our new beginnings knowing we are each an unfinished product. The charming expression of some of the more lighthearted traditional church folk sounds much the same. "Be patient with me," they say, "God isn't finished making me yet." And the tag line is, "...and God doesn't make junk!" Ah, yes. The cosmos—*LIFE*—isn't finished with any of us yet, nor are we finished with growing our souls and creating our *selves*.

Making it up as I go along

The high school student actors who joined an improvisation club were offered for purchase, tee shirts and sweatshirts identifying them as club members. The message on the shirts read, "I'm making this up as I go along." Aren't we all? I thought, and asked if a senior lady, long since graduated, could buy a shirt.

There is a story of New Year's festivity that I reported in my column when I wrote for the Burlington County NJ News-Press, which speaks to this miracle of creating ourselves as we go along. The owner of a small dress shop in a little town along the Delaware River told me about something that delighted her one New Year's Eve. It was 1966, and New Year's Eve fell on a Saturday. Mildred's Dress Shop was open the usual Saturday hours, and a shopper scurried in just before closing, wearing what appeared to be a robe (what we used to call a housecoat) and fuzzy slippers. Her hair was carefully coifed and her make-up artistic and complete. Beneath her robe, the lingerie was appropriate for formal wear. The lady quickly checked the racks and found a cocktail dress that pleased her. Taking silver dance slippers from her handbag, she donned gown and pumps, wrote a check, and with a huge smile, she slipped on her winter coat and left for the evening's celebration.

We regularly make decisions about how we will be, and who we will be as life progresses. This requires that you forgive yourself for anything you might have done or been in the past, recognize your capabilities and relax about your inabilities. The ancient Hebrew poets of Ecclesiastes have taught that everything has its season and its ripeness of time, and as you grow older your wisdom and experience must sometimes compensate for lessened physical excellence. So it is up to you to accept the best you have in you and to accept also the changes that may discomfort you.

There is in life an interdependence of joy and sorrow. A favorite quotation of my daughter Kristi is from my poem, "Reflections on the Resurgence of Joy." She has reminded me from time to time—in my own words, no less—*Indeed without the salt of many tears, I could not taste the sweet of candy canes... Praise be that life's not flat.* It has been said many different ways, and it is central to the Tao, the noble way. There is a balance in the cosmos that requires both darkness and light, for one could not exist without the other.

I can, I will, I have begun to...

As we choose our beginnings, we set goals for ourselves. Then it becomes necessary to turn mere goals into *intention* by moving from "I would like to," or "someday I want to," to "I will, I can, I have begun to..." Turning goals into intention requires that you articulate what you will do, make it known to others, believe in its inevitability, then do it!

Some years ago, I was receiving the mailings from the Church of Religious Science, as part of my professional reading. In January, the editor invited the readers to fill in a form printed in the publication. It was designed in a goals for the year format, and asked that the participants be quite specific and positive, writing their intentions as affirmations. Being a wordsmith, I pondered the exact form my goals would take, and I was very specific. Then I returned the completed form, enveloped with my name and address to the church office. One year later I received in the mail that same set of goals— written by my own hand. Two of the three were clearly accomplished and the third was under way. How? Why? It was because I was clear about my intention, and I was busy creating the me I would become, the life I would affirm.

I invite you now to take a few quiet moments to contemplate, not resolutions—those dreams so easily shattered—but your goals and intention. What do you really intend to become in the next week, the next month, the next year? How will you create a fullness of living for yourself? Write it down. The note of true intention will remind you: *Whatever you vividly imagine, ardently desire, sincerely believe, and enthusiastically act upon must inevitably come to pass.* You can help create yourself as you aspire to be, for every day is a new beginning.

Your hand holds the tiller.

Imagine, if you will, wind and white clouds, sun and sparkling water... white caps, perhaps, and a boat with a sail. Put your hand to the tiller and grasp the sheet—and you become at one with the elements and the craft that carries you. You are the sailboat; you are the wind; you are the sea. There's a scent of salt, or marshes, or pine trees around a lake, and sea birds, cormorants or loons... Peacefulness and excitement! A sense of going somewhere, and joy in the present moment, right where you are, and even an opportunity to dream. This kind of reverie is what comes of being a poet who is also a canvas sailor. For anyone who has sailed a boat of any size there is a magic in sailing that has in it excitement and tranquility, a celebrative, inspirational quality, and the lilt of poetry. It can be a momentous experience.

I learned to sail in a 12-foot Sunflower sailboat, on Beech Hill Pond in Maine. I'd grown up in New Jersey where the word pond indicated a small—very small—body of water, and a lake was somewhat larger. In Maine, however, I discovered the terms were defined quite differently. New England bodies of water are named according to their source, not their size, which in Maine is always quite large. A pond is spring fed, and a lake is stream fed. At Beech Hill Pond there was a westerly wind and a pounding surf. On a high weather day, we had waves to rival those at Newport Beach. The surrounding hills and forest, the shape of the pond and the resulting eddies and still spots challenged sailors to keep a weather eye and anticipate what might come next.

Growing up real

As a sailor and poet, I find the sailing metaphor particularly moving, and emotionally satisfying, and so I have chosen to tap the rich symbolism of sailing as a source for imagery to enhance our thinking on the subject of growth and change—growing up real.

When my son Mark graduated from high school, he wrote and delivered an essay on growing up— an affirmation of all that is best in childhood and a refusal to leave it behind as he moved forward into autonomy and authentic personhood. He spoke of the childlike creative spark and gift of imagination that allows us to see pictures in the clouds and hear laughter from the sea gulls, and he aspired to a life of responsibility and achievement charged with that same childlike energy and joy which he had known as a little boy. Recalling this lovely piece of work, I recognized that growing toward autonomy and authenticity, growing up real is a necessary part of our pathway to serenity.

Of sails and rudders

Dream with me of sailing that long-lost golden Sunflower on a sparkling summer's day. These are the metaphors that come to mind. Let's see your sailing forth as a voyage into growth, reaching for your ideals, your potential (your best self), and you will need both sails and rudder. You need sails for power, for energy and fortitude. You'll need them for inspiration. Rudderless, you would certainly sail in circles, go aground, or crash upon the rocks. You'll need the rudder for direction, motivation, autonomy, self-determination.

You will surely need an anchor as well, a safety provision that could keep you from going anywhere at all, if you let it have control. And then there is that vital force, the breath of life—the wind—without which boat and you would be totally becalmed. (I never fully appreciated the expression "that took the wind out of her sails," until I found myself "in irons," windless, on the water.) There is nothing so unmotivated as a sail or kite without a breeze.

In your life's journey your sails might represent personality, determination, skill, personal potency, intuition, creativity, and human relationships. Your rudder might be your intellect, logic, goals, sense of self and individuality. The anchor may be your heritage and tradition; it may be patience and faith. And the wind—that necessary "something" we may call God, Spirit, values, or our fathers' myths—those stories that symbolize the important things in the life of our families.

What were your father's dreams for himself and for you? Did he, like Judy Collins's father in the song "My Father" dream of Paris, and dancing and sailing on the Seine? Or like Tevye in *Fiddler on the Roof* did he dream of a great house with stairways going up and down, and one that's going nowhere just for show...if I were a wealthy man. Did your father dream of the great things he might do for the world, or of the honors your deeds would bestow? Did he perhaps long for time to play with you, and sadly, foolishly, spend his time instead working to buy you things? What were the values expressed in the stories our fathers told us and in the lives they lived?

My father and my uncle who was like a father or older brother to me, were both gentle, loving, laughing men who danced with me at the New Year's Eve Charity Ball in my hometown. When I was a little sprite, Papa sang to me and gave me wooden curls to wear as I watched him plain a two-by-four. And Unkie played games with me, took me riding in his car, and made me laugh. I learned from them that life is worth celebrating; that honesty and honor are essential; that kindness is the way we behave toward everyone; that I can do anything I put my mind to.

And from the family myths what did I learn? Papa was the hero of one family myth, and it was all about how easy-going and even-tempered he was until he was pushed too far. From this story of my father and other tales I learned that gentleness, patience, and forbearance are the hallmarks of power.

The gifts of wholeness my father and mother and all who nurtured and guided me have bestowed are the sails and rudder of my human authenticity. Like the skin horse in *The Velveteen Rabbit*, the nurturing parent-figures of my life taught me I could grow up real, if I chose not to break too easily, not to allow myself sharp edges or to need to be too carefully kept. "Real" is authentically beautiful. To be real is to dare to be autonomous, retaining wonder and surprise—the joyousness of childhood—even as we gain understanding. To be real is to reach out to one another in mutuality and love, combining reason and intuition, thinking and feeling, so we are whole. It is to recognize our failings, shortcomings, neglects and failures, and to go on from there with hope and faith and determination.

EVER YOUNG

Life is rich with simple pleasure.
Peace and beauty beyond measure
Light my days if I but listen
in the stillness of my soul.

Each day offers new surprises,
Herbs and flowers and bright sunrises
That refresh my mind
and soften ills and pain I can't control.

In the quiet I awaken
To successful paths I've taken,
Not mistakes or failures as I thought—
because they brought me here.

Here - the place of grace and truth,
Integrity and health and youth
Expressed in song and laughter,
a denial of the my years.

Carry the flame.

We swim in the river of life. As the philosopher Heraclites taught, we cannot step in the same river twice. We, like the river, are ever changing—new every minute! Ninety-eight percent of the atoms of our bodies are replaced in the course of one year. Our skeleton—that apparently permanent and unchanging hat rack on which our body hangs— actually undergoes an almost complete transition every three months, and even the mountains and rocks under our feet shift in a never-ending dance through time. The real miracle of change is that you can create it as you plunge into living. You can make your world in the very present moment, by the way you choose to perceive it, by the way you choose to live in it.

I was listening to the country-western radio station the other day, on my way over the freeways, and the DJ invited listeners to text in their latest jokes to be shared on the air. He then delivered what sounded at first like a serious announcement: "Due to the current social, economic, moral, and political situation in the country, the light at the end of the tunnel has been extinguished."

On first reading this, we're startled, then we chuckle. But think about it a minute—what kind of belief system would allow that kind of so-called solution? Do we extinguish the light at the end of the tunnel, or do we kindle an illumination of our own as we make the crossing? I opt for some better advice from a friend, "Carry the light, carry the lamp, carry the flame!

Being a carrier of light is a matter of attitude. Therapist Barry Kaufman tells a story about Edward, a client who complained of three things that deeply disturbed him. First, his career was stalled; second, his marriage was floundering and filled with friction; and finally, his sexual potency was at rock bottom. Edward decided he would see solving even one of the three as a major success.

At first Edward blamed his wife for being cold and contributing to his sexual problems; but bit-by-bit he remembered his love for her in spite of their problems. Rediscovering this love didn't solve anything, but it did make him feel just a tad better.

"Life is unfair!" he said, but then he laughed and decided that since fighting the universe (the unfairness of life) didn't solve anything, he wanted to stop fighting. "Doc Kaufman," he said, "my business issues aren't resolved, but I've shifted my position a bit and somehow I'm feeling better"

Discussing the sexual problems, Edward recognized his own beliefs and judgments about sex and aging and his lowered expectations. Then he noted some of the advantages of growing older and listed for himself some of the new activities he now enjoyed.

At this point, Edward told Dr. K. that he was feeling really good. "The issues are the same," he said, "but I'm not letting those problems be as important." Nothing had changed; and yet everything had changed.

It's amazing what happens when our thinking changes! Thoughts and the feelings they create have an immediate and powerful effect on reality, changing even the chemistry of our bodies in an instant. Change comes from the decision to change— in an instant. Flexibility and growth enable us to meet change with equanimity.

Innovators use change as a challenge to achieve further growth and accomplishment. A black and white approach to every question will leave you with a gray tweed life when you could have a rainbow. When you find yourself in a rut, and things aren't working, it is necessary to go outside your usual pattern. Break loose from habit and go beyond imagined limits and restrictions. Welcome change and see how you will grow!

...Write! my heart demands

Chapter Eight

Mindfulness Meadow

Be here now.

Life Is…

Life is good. I posted this upon my desktop.
Life is wild. I watch the circus passing, non-stop.
Life is rich. So much to learn, so much to live for,
So many friends to meet, so much to give for.
Life is fun. The days and nights alight with laughter.
Life is hopeful. Joy is ours "forever after."
Life is sad, but we have learned to find the lesson,
The gift of light in darkness, and the blessing.
Life is ours to celebrate, appreciate and sing of.
My wish for you—
may each day shine with joy and bring love.

Letting go—

I heard recently about a fellow named Henry who
was a Sierra Club enthusiast. Henry was out hiking
in a mountainous area when suddenly the earth

broke away from under his feet, opening a chasm beneath him. Henry madly flung his arms out and part way down, grabbed a bush, holding himself momentarily from falling thousands of feet into the void. "Help!" he screamed. "Is anybody up there?"

Amazingly, the heavens opened up and a bright light shone upon him. A beautiful mellifluous voice spoke. "Henry," said the voice. "This is God, Henry. I am all that is good and loving and meaningful. Let go of the bush, Henry, and I will save you. Let go." Henry clung to that bush for another minute or so, and then he called out, "Is there anybody else up there?"

Can you, perhaps, identify with Henry? Letting go is hard. It may be the hardest spiritual challenge you'll ever meet. Let go friend! And be in the now. When there is no cure for the situation, your only chance of healing may come from letting go. Let go of ingrained ideas and unrealistic expectations. Let go of demanding too much of yourself or of others. Let go of annoyance and resentment. You cause yourself great unnecessary pain by too great an attachment to your own expectations, images, and standards.

One elderly lady I knew was very unhappy because her grown grandsons did not live up to her expectations of them. She believed they should stop by at their grandparents' house once or twice a week and do whatever strenuous chores their granddad could no longer do himself. That would have been very nice—regular acts of kindness rather than the random kind. But that was *her* dream, her image of the way things should be, not theirs.

Because she was disappointed in her expectations, and refused to let go, she was an angry lady and very unhappy. *Let go of the bush, Grandmother, and the cosmos will catch you.* Or you could even let go of your pride and ask the grandsons to do some specific task. They might surprise you with their willingness to help.

If you fret and fuss because those with whom you live or closely associate don't live up to your standards and ideals of behavior; if you allow yourself to suffer pain because they fall short of hospitality or thoughtfulness, courtesy or warmth, then you will suffer unnecessarily by your own choice. Live this moment fully, tasting its essence, allowing yourself to experience transcendent joy even when in the midst of sorrow. When you hold yourself tied to old fears, angers, and burdens, you squander the present and build yourself a prison fashioned from your own emotions. If on the other hand you recognize your feelings, honor them and let them go, you can be effective in the very present moment.

The power of white-water rafting

Control is a primary western cultural value, and letting go is especially difficult for us in the U S. To go with the flow just isn't our way. We probably don't have the advantage of a Taoist or Buddhist upbringing that teaches how to "go white-water rafting through life." The western way is to jet boat. We love our power and speed, and we believe the river is the enemy to be conquered. We roar along untouched by the nature of things and so avoid touching reality. It's all just great—the noise and the smell of the engine—until we run out of gas or something shuts down the motor. Where is our power then? Who is in charge of our life's journey if our plans go awry?

Maybe we could learn something from those folks in the yellow rubber boats moving along on the current. There is no way they'll go against the flow, as our jet boater loves to do. But they aren't powerless, either. The white-water rafter studies the rapids, calculates the force of the water as it goes around obstacles, and decides how to use the power of the river to go in a natural direction. It's an exciting, satisfying, and ecologically sound way they travel, and they don't have to worry about equipment breakdown nor wonder who is in charge of the trip.

Letting go is not closing your mind to life. It is living fully in the now. It is being aware and mindful of the little things that make life so miraculous.

Be fully present.

There is a small anonymously written greeting card verse that begins:

> You wake up in the morning, and lo!
> your purse is magically filled

with twenty-four hours of the
unmanufactured tissue of
of your life. It is yours. . .

Your time is yours to invest with living, loving,
giving, doing, being. You can choose how you will
live your minutes and days—you can choose to be
here now, to claim your time—your treasure. How
do you mold and use that vital, vibrant, crackling
passage of time? How do you create it, manage it, fill
it, savor it? What will you do with the richness of time
that is your own precious possession, in the *resident
sacredness of the present moment?* How will you live in
it? What are the attitudes and techniques that enable
some people to empower their lives, take control of
their time, and create their desired outcomes?

Time is, after all, an artificial construct—a lie we tell
ourselves about reality. We humans have replaced
the rhythms of the natural world around us and
the rhythms of our own bodies with clocks and
calendars, timelines and linear history. We pretend
that we can save time. What does that mean? You
can't accumulate time in a storehouse. It makes no
sense to want to save up existence, when existence
is created by being spent.

By choosing to be happy only in memory or
expectation, you can be but dimly aware of the
present, even when the present is full of the good
you've been seeking. If preoccupation with the past or
the future makes you less alive in the present—think
about it—are you actually living in the real world?

There is a lovely ritual of mindfulness described by Thich Nhat Hanh. I recognize that such an activity is extremely difficult to schedule, especially for young mothers, but perhaps finding the time will be worth the effort. This is how to begin: "In the morning, after you have cleaned and straightened up your house, or in the afternoon, after you have worked in the garden or watched clouds or gathered flowers, prepare a pot of tea to sit and drink while fully aware."

Pay attention, don't gulp down your tea as if it might be snatched away in the next instant. Don't treat it like a quick cup of coffee swallowed during a work break. Drink your tea with pleasure and appreciation—drink slowly, evenly, without rushing toward the future. Live the actual moment. Only this actual moment is real. Don't be concerned with the future. Don't worry about things you have to do. Don't think about something missed. Savor the tea; savor your quiet moments. And remember, you have to be present to win.

In the fullness of time

Here's a lovely phrase: *in the fullness of time.* Every action, each choice or decision, each step in our becoming and creating has its own special time. There is a time when it is necessary to move beyond a dead-end job, a lifeless relationship, a house or apartment or room that stifles your creativity or surrounds you with clutter, or cold neatness, chaos, or loneliness. There is a time to move forward, and we know instinctively when our times for change arrive. This kind of time is not linear or other-directed. It is inner directed and intuited—the *appropriate* time.

And only in the now—in the dawn of a new consciousness—do we begin to initiate, to stimulate, and refuse to wait. Only in the now do we begin to make life move with us as we claim our right to choose how we shall use our time.

The days and weeks as we usually view them—the time in your comfortable, stable Day-runner—is linear and sequential; the seasons are cyclical or spiral time; and the mystery of the cosmos is timeless. History is a story we tell, whether it is our own story or that of nations, tribes or families. One wag wrote: "Life is what happens to you when you're making other plans." I reply:

Life is this very minute,
this breath, this smile,
this tear, this laughter.
Life is now and the now
creates its own tomorrow.
Each today rests
on the structure designed
and built through many yesterdays,
yet only this sacred present moment is real.

Be aware.

Be here now. Look at the person in line behind you in the grocery store, the one in the motorized cart, or the one with several small kiddies tagging along. Be aware. He may need help unloading the shopping basket, or maybe just a pleasant greeting, and the smile you'll earn by helping or saying hello is as good for your health as the exercise bending to transfer the groceries must be. Many people feel invisible because they are old or don't stand out or meet the criteria for glamor, and by being self-absorbed or preoccupied you will reinforce that sad evaluation. Don't let the person beside you be invisible. Be awake. Take notice. Say hello, perhaps, or "Can I help you with that?"

Give your presence as a present.

An old high school friend noted the many change of address cards I'd sent throughout the years and dubbed me a gypsy. My house-to-house gypsy life has taught me, however, to travel light. It has made me aware of how little it takes to make a home. What is required is my presence, my aesthetic sense, and my love—heart room and hyacinths. Wherever I am fully present, there is peace, there is home!

Doing ministry in a small penniless suburban congregation leaves the pastor (often a woman) with no choice but to work two full-time jobs. There are, after all, no part-time ministries, only part-time remunerations. So the reverend person must often find a worldly source of sustaining income. We do something that has been called a *tentmaker ministry*— referring back to desert preachers of old—one in which the preacher must also work at some other trade to survive economically.

One of my many tentmaker employments was as guru and office organizer to the psychologist, Michael Riskin. Michael often said my biggest gift to him was *being there*. Coining a new and appropriate word for the help I provided, he remarked that I *inspirited* him. The loving connection, the being with, requires us to listen, to put ourselves in touch with one another, to simply *be*. And to give the gift of total attention, to give our presence as a present.

Even in sorrow...

To be in the moment, when disappointed, sad or troubled, you must experience even the sadness fully. Acknowledge sad feelings, honor them and let them go. Being here in the present I look a bit more deeply into my own missed targets:

On writing .....or not. (Not a poem!)
Why aren't you writing? Have you stopped thinking?
Good God, no. I may have stopped writing
because I can't stop thinking.
It keeps me awake nights, this busy buzz in my head
And nothing profitable comes of it.
I plan projects, rearrange furniture,
plot ways to avoid financial disaster.
And none of it goes beyond the darkness
of my bedroom quiet.
Next morning I walk the dog, check the mail,
take my senior meds...
And read
and read
and read...

avoiding TV stories I can't quite hear
clearly enough to scan or understand.
Write! my colleagues urge me.
Write! my son entreats.
Write! my heart demands...
And when one sad poem slips past my careful sadness
filter
I hesitate to share, though sharing is my life's blood.
Don't want sad!
Don't need tears.
Don't like this...
But I write. I write.

Then I share "the sad" in the moment and even
sadness becomes serene...

Struggle
I read and read to fill the empty hours.
My eyes reach for vision
Through viscous film and tears.
My heart longs for connections
And the warmth of human touch.
Alone, day after day I yearn
For ordinary words remembered
From the times not long ago,
My home so full of youth—of
Busy voices, joy and laughter.
I remind myself that I am not alone,
Recollect that all the world is one.
And struggle to rejoice in this again
As one small dog reminds me I am blessed
With love, forever life's most precious gift.

Here is a joyful discovery. Anxiety cannot exist in the present moment. I learned this basic truth in a human sexuality class (of all places!) and I have found it valuable in every part of my life. In the set of exercises called *sensate focus* we learn to be here now in the manner of Buddhists—to become fully aware of our senses in the present to the exclusion of all else. Being tuned in to your eyes and ears and nose, your elbows, knees and toes, your palms and fingertips—feeling every tiny touch, you cannot think about what might be going to happen (or not happen) in the immediate or distant future. If you are fully in the now, you cannot worry yourself about what may be or might have been in the future or the past. You cannot accommodate anxiety! Be here now!

. . .something called simplicity

Chapter Nine

Tranquility Pond

Cultivate inner quiet.

Quiet...

We search for peace and quiet
Here amid the roar of trucks,
*   the boom and beat,*
The passing sounds of stereo
*   too bold for human ear.*
All this we hear
*   that shatters peace and quiet.*

We yearn for simple sounds...
Cool breeze that stirs the leaves,
*   a child's sweet laughter,*
The refrain of trickling water in a fount,
A summer rain, love's murmurs
*   soft and quiet.*

Let's turn the volume down
And watch the garden shapes and hues

the passing birds,
or neighbors on the path.
Regale ourselves with stars at night
    or clouds at noon
Instead of noise—We may discover
peace and quiet.

In the silence you can nurture the thoughts leading to deeper understanding. Here is a favorite piece of New England wisdom: *Speak only when what you have to say is an improvement on silence*

George Eliot said, "Blessed is the man who, having nothing to say, abstains from giving, in words, evidence of the fact."

Clear out the clutter.

Life is absurd in many ways. Living wisely, living nobly, living joyfully and humanely is not easy in the day-to-day struggles of the real world. Yet our values and the very search for meaning that brings us on this journey demand that we reach toward that goal. And so we struggle, intending to live our ideals and frequently falling short in the confusion of a world that sometime doesn't make sense, a world full of ambiguity and illogic, a world too full of noise and clutter.

There is in all of us a yearning for something better in ourselves and in the world. Some call that something perfection, but perhaps that's too illusive for us mere mortals. So let's call our goal "the good" or the ideal.

There is also in us a need to make order out of the chaos. We ponder life's confusions, and we try to make a system, a logical process out of what we see, or think we see. Just as we order our rooms we will order our lives.

Finding your inner quiet will be much more difficult, even impossible, if you live amid clutter and chaos. "How," you may wonder, "can I avoid the messy household, office, or garage that hints at a messy mind?" The answer to that appeared at the book's beginning as we prepared for our merry trip—start by getting organized.

To start organizing:

- clear you mind
- clear the stage,
- clear the floors and tabletops,
- empty chairs, closets, boxes,
- give away,
- throw away,
- put away...

And never, but never leave your stuff* (towels, dirty clothes, books and toys, tangled wires, papers—you name it) scattered on the floor! * *Stuff* - with a shout out to George Carlin.

Now, think about the way you do your best work, what you use and need near at hand. You've surely heard "a place for everything and everything in its place," and you ignore that wisdom at your own peril. Once you have sorted through the stuff that surrounds you and sifted out that which is worth keeping, find for everything you've decided to keep a place to live, its own special place. Then whenever you have used something, put it back where it belongs. You'll be amazed how much simpler and easier life becomes and how much more effective you become.

A lovely setting cultivates calm.

At the heart of beauty is something called simplicity. It is spare and neat, without excess. As you move toward serenity, you will discover the effects of beauty on your mood and accomplishments.

Surrounding yourself with color and light, with simplicity and order, with lovely things to look at will make you more effective and give you deep satisfaction. A single blossom in a small jar or bottle can lift your spirits and cheer a room.

Gloom is all too easily spread, so open the blinds and let in the sun or turn on a table lamp (overheads are often harsh and troubling to the spirit.) Play soothing or cheerful music, hang a picture that pleases you, light a scented candle or open a window to freshen the air.

Unburden yourself.

When helping my dear friend's sons to sort and distribute her household goods in the aftermath of her death, I became aware once more of the disruption that invades life when we lose touch with simplicity. When we are suffocated by excessive belongings, smothered by too much of anything, we bog down in an emotional swamp. The noise of confusion and clutter drowns out inner quiet.

When I returned to my own study after that visit to the home of my lost friend, I sorted all my furniture, home goods and kitchenware to see what I could spare, and phoned a charity pickup to call for them. Then, remembering notes too personal to share found in the dear lady's desk, I re-read my twelve bound journals, the stories of my life. Among the poems and memories of sweet delights, I had written of poverty, struggles and pain—too much sorrow to leave behind. Personal grief, pain-filled moments, heavy emotions and expressions of sexuality need not be left behind to further burden those already bereaved. I kept the writings worthy of sharing and destroyed the rest.

Stop. Breathe...

Stop. Sit quietly for a moment or two. Breathe. Listen to the rhythms of your own body, the song of birds, the breeze in the willow, the whisper of rain or the sparkling notes of a wind chime. Smile. OK, so you don't have a wind chime and it hasn't rained here in weeks. Breathe anyway. . .you get the idea.

An artist friend once gifted me with a beautiful piece of calligraphic art in which she presented the word

Aloha writ large. The O, she filled with swirls of color, which might represent the music of the spheres or sunlit rainbows on the ocean waves. Beneath the word Aloha, in smaller letters she'd penned: "Alo— in the presence of, Ha—the breath of God." In our quiet moments as we pause to breathe, to taste the breath of life, we are all blessed to be in the presence of the breath of God. Another of my friends pointed out that breathing is *Being* and the verb *I am* in French is *j'suis*, which echoes the name of Jesus. Every breath is a breath of life, of being.

The path of paradox

A precious gift purchased with a little girl's saved-up pennies, was a small plaque painted with these words from Emerson:

> *Do not follow where the path may lead.*
> *Go, instead, where there is no path, and leave a trail.*

Perhaps my trail is the path of paradox.

I'm aware that I superimpose my little systems on reality to create hopeful positive designs of order. For me, one possibility among life's many fragile and tentative answers in the search for meaning is akin to the Taoist yin and yang, or to Carl Jung's concept of wholeness created by opposites. Perhaps the very qualities in each of us that seem to be irreconcilable opposites are in reality two sides of the same wholeness.

Years ago—fairly early in my ministry, in fact—I began to explore the idea that my version of the Tao, the way of harmony, might be called the path of paradox. There is in the yin and yang a harmony or unity of opposites that creates wholeness, and it is in that spirit I began to look at certain paradoxical ideas.

According to Lao-tzu, the great Taoist teacher, the harmony that has naturally existed between heaven and earth from the beginning can be found by anyone at any time. He tells us life is not a setter of traps, but a teacher of valuable lessons. By learning from, appreciating, and working with whatever happens in everyday life, we can create harmony and happiness. The Taoist approach is this—through working in harmony with life's circumstances, by metaphorically "white water rafting" or dancing to the rhythms of life, we can change what others see as negative into something positive, change the overwhelming into the manageable.

My explorations of this concept grew out of a somewhat extraordinary experience I had not long after coming to California. Within a period of no more than two weeks, the same strange thought or evaluation was voiced to me by perhaps six different people, in six very differing circumstances. The settings ranged from responding to one of my sermons, or being in deep conversation, to sharing one of my newly written poems or dancing together. The individuals each said to me, "You make me feel peaceful.... and excited."

Peaceful and excited—isn't that a contradiction? What are these people really saying to me? As I lived with this new bit of interpersonal input, I came to realize that this was indeed a description of my way of being in the world, a kind of shorthand for my ministry and the goals I hoped to achieve: peaceful and exciting, passionate and serene, comforting and inspiring, challenging and supportive.

From this first acceptance of my personal paradox, I began to look at some of the others in my life. I discovered the sweet marriage of vulnerability and strength. I knew that I was both vulnerable and strong, and I further knew that without real strength I would not have the courage to allow myself vulnerability; I would have built a fortress to protect my own weaknesses.

Journaling paradox

In my journal I wrote:

Vulnerable, you call me—open and risking. And I pondered whether this indeed were so. The vulnerability, I know, was always here inside of me, but the draperies on my windows were my smiles, the bolt on my door, keeping the vulnerable me inside and intruders out, was what you call my talent, skills and capabilities. As I have grown these last few years, I learned the bolt and the door could be opened. The skills could be used to take me outside to meet others, rather than hiding me.

I am indeed, like all of us, an enigma and a paradox, a hyphenated self with opposites ever at play in my person. Even as I have been depicted as peaceful and exciting, I am vulnerable and strong. It is in the transparency I impart to these conditions that there is a change. The vulnerability was always there, the fears, and the acute awareness of my own frailty and imperfection. Yet I felt I had to mask the fears and pain with smiles and competence. I had to brave it through.

And perhaps I still do. But there are those who look through my windows and see that I am both strong and vulnerable, and who make of that no mystery, for it is such a human thing. We live with ambiguity always...and we only slowly start to understand that life's contradictions are in reality the full-bodied music of the joy of living.

Learn to enjoy your own company.

Throughout my adult life the homes I have made were filled with young people—my children, their friends and the children of high school drama departments, church youth groups, the neighbors. My house was affectionately known as Dori's Dorm. When my four children were grown and left to establish homes of their own I found myself living alone for the first time and I felt loneliness for the first time. I began to loath the lovely townhouse I had rented, for I had yet to learn how to enjoy solitude and to appreciate my own company.

So I moved once more to a house with a garden on a tree-lined terrace. After finding my tranquil space, I at last discovered I had been blessed with resources for inner peace. I have always loved reading and had a gift for writing. As I write a thoughtful essay, craft the lean richness of a poem or read a good book, I discover bits of myself that make me really good company. Solitary and at peace amid my inner quiet, I awaken to the oneness of the universe and know that I am not alone.

You, too, might meet yourself and enjoy the pleasure of your own good company on the pages of a journal, in your dreams or in moments of meditation. Enter your inner quiet through alpha consciousness. Breathe in the breath of life, and call up mind pictures of the most tranquil and beautiful places you can remember or imagine.

Pictures are the language of the mind and there is no such word as "no" within the unconscious, so employ only "Yes Talk." The mind doesn't hear the negative, the "no" or the "won't." It misinterprets "I won't get angry" as an affirmation of anger, but fully understands "I will remain tranquil." Nurture positive thoughts and fill your heart with "Yes!"

To find quiet and tranquility in the midst of a busy day carry it within you and discover it in the beauty of simple tasks.

Works of My Hands

Chop wood, carry water,
Work is sacred, sages say.
Bake bread, smooth linen,
Ancient truths inform today.
Pot plants, sweep carpets,
Beauty in a single bloom.
Thought stilled, heart mindful
As I rearrange a room.
Sunlight, favored music,
Till serenity expands.
All life is hallowed
By the labors of my hands.

. . . moving along in San Francisco

CHAPTER TEN

Enthusiasm Park

Be passionate; get excited!

Light up the space!

In theatre lore they tell us
"Good luck" must not be said,
So thespians encourage friends
With "break a leg" instead.

The maestro knows, however,
Of the power of a smile
As it becomes a beacon
To enchant and to beguile.

He knows this craft is more than luck.
It's skill and work and choice,
And sending forth the writer's truth.
And so he lifts his voice…

Inspiring the actor's art—
Life, energy and grace
Igniting incandescence
As he calls, "Light up the space!"

Serenity and passion are not opposites nor mutually exclusive, but rather interdependent and supportive. Passion is the light of a torch, not the fire of destruction. Passion is an ardent belief. It is love infused with magnificent energy that can make our dreams a viable reality. It is the nuts and bolts day-to-day work of getting going, and the enthusiasm and energy you bring to that work!

Ralph Waldo Emerson wrote: *Every great and commanding movement in the annals of the world is a triumph of enthusiasm. Nothing great was ever achieved without it*

I've been told that we can all change our lives for the better in just one month, if we are daring enough, outrageous enough, to do this little exercise every morning for thirty days. Please put your book aside, stand up and jump up and down three times, shouting each time, "I'm excited! I'm excited; I'm excited!" Pretty silly, isn't it? But think about it. Who would you feel more drawn to, the weary, bored and boring people who find life a drag, or the bright-eyed and lively ones who are excited and even a bit outrageous? By reason of their own enthusiasm, these people are not just excited, they are exciting!

Dancing through life

The TV news is not often pleasant, and very rarely is it happy, but one night the evening news carried a story of a lady whose dream of 60 years had just been realized. This wonderful little lady, on reaching the estimable age of one hundred and four finally got to travel to San Francisco and ride on one of the famous trolley cars. As she stepped briskly off the picturesque vehicle, reporters asked her to share her secret for such a long and satisfying life. She answered simply, "You've gotta *keep moving!*"

Keep your mind and your spirit in motion even if your body is a little slow. Keep moving, it's the key to staying young, a recipe for health and fitness, a source of energy, an answer to the needs of businesses, of organizations, or of individuals in search of serenity—let life be a dance!

Have you tuned into the difference between just plain old folks and the vibrant, elegant elders like the lady moving along in San Francisco? All of us know some people barely in their middle years that we think of as old. Henry David Thoreau said, "None are so old as those who have outlived enthusiasm." I fear these old young people have never had enough enthusiasm to outlive.

To be in harmony

During the thirty years before the beginning of the Common Era and a few years into the time we date the first century, a Jewish religious leader, philosopher, and scholar named Hillel the Elder flourished. He is credited with this strange and somewhat esoteric piece of wisdom:

> *If we are not for ourselves, who will be for us?*
> *If we are for ourselves only; what are we?*
> *If not now; when?*

What might this mean for you, today? Is it, perhaps, a small treasure map, a coded message for a better, more passionate life? Is it a secret spiritual clue to something you really ought to consider?

I see in these ancient words from Judaism an echo of Navajo wisdom and a suggestion of my own Relational Panentheism. For the Navajo *Dinee* (a word that translates "the people") human prosperity and peace of mind depend on harmony with the powers running the natural world, and harmony with self and with one another. And I believe my spiritual center revolves around these three relationships:

- to the cosmos, the divine, the *One*,
- to myself, my inner core, my peace of mind,
- to you, my brothers and sisters.

If we are not for ourselves, who will be for us? What does it mean to be for ourselves? My guess is that it means in part, to tell your story, to be willing to speak up about your beliefs and your dreams for a better world. It means taking responsibility for your choices. It means getting excited about your goals and values.

If we are for ourselves only, what are we? To be for more than yourself you might be required (to the best of your ability) to do justice as an agent of love and mercy, and to walk humbly with your neighbors, while living your ideals with passion.

I believe simple kindness can make the world better, and that is not a wimpy belief. It isn't easy to be always, in all ways, kind. It is not simple to spread that kindness. But that is my vision and my dream. What is your vision, your dream? Do you or do you not believe that good and dedicated persons can change the world? You have to understand and be passionately committed to the dream, the vision, in order to share it and make it come true.

Humility

During a panel discussion of humanism and theism a member of the panel delivered a tirade against religious language that made her uncomfortable. Although we in the clergy are called to comfort the afflicted and afflict the comfortable, she wanted her comfort back. A man in the audience then made a long speech that ended in an explosion of fury over being told from the pulpit that there are things that are unknowable. I was so startled, that I asked him if he actually believed that through his reasoning he knew everything. And *he said yes*! Obviously one thing he did not know was the meaning of *hubris*—overweening pride that sees the self as omniscient.

Bridging the reality gap

For many years I longed with a passion to plumb the depths of reality, to bridge what I thought of as the reality gap. Our life experience can appear to be either order or chaos, reason or emotion, permanence or change; yet *reality* lies always somewhere between.

In the spirit of open inquiry, intuitive discovery, and self-reliance I determined to explore reality as the space between. Let's struggle with this together. What is the nature of reality? This is a question asked by philosophers throughout the ages. It has been asked by scientists, theologians, poets, playwrights, and artists. And their conclusions are far from unanimous, or even harmonious.

Consider first the conflicting aspects of reality such as rational thought and emotion, consistency and inconsistency. Ralph Waldo Emerson and Tom Robbins both urge us to accept life's absurdities and move beyond a "petty consistency;" but for the orderly mind that's not an easy task.

A light-hearted quotation from Liza Minnelli says, "Reality is something you rise above." And that stirred this poet to respond:

> *Reality is the product of the mind's knowing,*
> *the body's sensing*
> *and the affective—heart's felt—understanding.*
> *Reality is a mystery and a miracle.*

It is unique and indescribable to and with
each individual.
Your reality is your own.

Examine, if you will, the tools with which we create or co-create our reality. We use:

- Opinion - Although usually couched in terms of fact and "the way it is," opinion is actually made up of emotion, judgment, and the effects of your personal background.
- Knowledge, which uses your database of fact and sensory information and can sometimes, be deceiving.
- Belief, which is made up of assumptions and values and expresses itself in what you do, the way you actually live. Any so-called belief belied by your behavior is merely what you profess and meaningless.

Finally, sprinkle in these thoughts:

- Absolutes are an illusion; there's always so much more to be considered. (This is the "Let's face it, we don't have all the answers or even all the questions," aspect of reality.)
- Reality encompasses absurdities and contradictions as well as an exquisite kind of order.

I believe in the harmony...
    and the dissonance of the cosmos.
I believe in life's absurdity...
    and its order.

And I believe in the human family—
Our wisdom and folly, cruelty and care,
Our imperfection and divine potential
As men and women, brothers and sisters.
I long for a world that never was—
Just and nurturing to all people,
Tender and supportive toward all that lives.
And I believe it is worth the struggle
To work toward building that world.
It is worth the risk
To reach out to others
In human kindness.
I believe in the energy and inspiration
That creates beauty
And opens doorways
To ever-changing truths.
I believe in love.

- Human wholeness is created by the interplay of reason, intuition, and emotion, body and soul. We build our reality with our combined senses, emotions and accumulated experience.

How do you describe your reality?

Your perceptions and assumptions create and change your reality. Remember the folk story of the blind men and the elephant in which the unseen creature was variously described as a tree, a rope, a snake, or a carpet. Each of us lives isolated in our own perceptual and experiential world, a fact that makes communication at best difficult, if not impossible. We build bridges of metaphor to reach across the isolation and touch. But we each describe our reality differently.

How could we expect to describe reality in the same way, when our judgments and perceptions are so varied? Suppose you experience your kitchen to be an absolute mess, yet a friend finds it "kind of homey and lived-in with just those few dishes and newspapers around." Is your description wrong, or is your friend's a lie? Is it one of those wonderful overcast opal days or gloomy, cold, and depressing? Is it crisp and invigorating or too dang cold? It is for each of us just what we perceive it to be.

You will find what you expect to find.

There were two Episcopal priests who had a long-running disagreement over a habit of one of them. He was known for smoking during prayers and his colleague disapproved. The two finally decided to take their disagreement to the Bishop. Each put the problem before His Grace in private, and each came out from the meeting having been confirmed in his original position. How could that happen? It went something like this. The first priest, the one who objected to his colleague's nasty habit, asked the Bishop if it was appropriate to smoke while praying, and the ecclesiastic authority responded that it was not. Then the smoker met with the Bishop and asked him if it was appropriate to pray while smoking, and the reply was a heartfelt YES.

Whatever you believe deep down, even unconsciously, filters out all the wonderful potentialities of your individual universe, leaving only what you expect. You will see what you look for!

I read somewhere that Claudette Colbert, speaking about the use of makeup, said "It matters more what's in a woman's face than what's on it." It is clear that the life we live shows upon our faces, and here is that idea taken a little further:

Even as we create our faces,
we create our lives...
by the beliefs we hold,
the "good" or "bad" we expect,
the beauty or ugliness we seek.

Whatever we are seeking...
expecting...convinced we will find...
we will indeed encounter.
And isn't it a shock to realize
it's there because
we always knew it would be.

Your experience of reality conforms to the manner in which you observe it. There is a scientific parable that illustrates this truth—once again using the imagery of the blind observer. The blind woman *sees* the snowflake as water, because her manner of observation—touch—melts the flake. And it has been proven in the laboratories that energy traveling hundreds of light years since its inception can be changed from waves to particles or from particles to waves by the manner in which it is perceived.

It has been said there are always portions of our hearts into which no one is able to enter, even if we invite them. This speaks to the great difficulty we face as we attempt communication— *For every human personality is at last a mystery and a secret, locked away from every other living soul by the failure of language to bridge our isolation and unlock the oneness of the cosmos. Tiny windows of the spirit open us to one another as we peer through the translucent metaphors, which only begin dimly to reveal the commonality of the human experience.*

It is not just with our eyes that we see nor with our ears that we hear, but with the heart—that intuitive inner self—that we recognize ourselves in one another. My passion, the part of my life that always ignites my enthusiasm, is my writing. I feel intense pleasure as the words begin to grace the empty page. I thrill to share what I have written, and joyously give the work life by sending it into the world of readers. Having traveled to Canada and Mexico, to Germany, Switzerland, France, Holland and Norway, I merrily claim the status of *internationally* unknown poet. I find even such silliness exciting, and delight in celebrating my vast anonymity.

What skills or simple pleasures can you profess, applaud and launch with verve? Enthusiastically tell the world! Get excited!

Look, Mommy, look!

CHAPTER ELEVEN

Beauty Bay

Honor & Share Beauty.

after the rain

pounding rain
a glowering sky
        then suddenly so bright
what message is life sending now
as sparkling leaves
bow to the breeze
        amid the dazzling light

moving shadows
dancing sun
        mood-shift from gold to gray
then back to silver edging clouds
and hearts that sing
as birds take wing
        life's magical today

Although Henri Matisse was nearly 28 years younger than Auguste Renoir, the two great artists were steadfast friends and often spent time together. Renoir lived to be 78, and during the last years of his life he was confined to his home, almost paralyzed with arthritis. Matisse visited him daily. Auguste Renoir, in spite of his infirmities continued to paint until shortly before his death—fourteen years after he was stricken with the crippling arthritis. One day, during Renoir's long struggle with the disease, Matisse became so saddened by his friend's pain that he spoke out and asked, "Auguste, why do you continue to paint when every brush stroke is achieved only through an agony of pain?" Renoir answered very simply, "The pain passes; the beauty remains."

The beauty remains. Beauty, that awe inspiring gift of the universe, lasts and outshines pain. It dims images of cruelty, ugliness, and squalor. Beauty remains— at the center of deep human spiritual values. Truth and beauty are honored in poetry, in the public domain, in the privacy of the heart and the nurture of the spirit. Johann von Goethe said, "Every day look at a beautiful picture, read a beautiful poem, listen to some beautiful music, and if possible, say some reasonable thing." What he may have been telling us is that the very act of immersing ourselves in beauty will make it not merely possible, but finally inevitable to say and do the reasonable thing.

Feast upon beauty.

Bathe your eyes in beauty; offer beauty to all your senses; it will create within you an inner beauty that expresses itself in nobility, gentleness and courage. A friend and one of my spiritual guides offered me this piece of wisdom: "Only that which you take in are you able to express to the world." The rule of inflow and outflow is very clear. Only if you choose to absorb beauty, do you have beauty to give.

We encounter beauty in many ways in every place we choose to find it. There is music in the wind or the song of rain, beauty in the silken touch of a baby's fingers, or a kitten's ears, beauty in the scent of new mown hay, the taste of strawberries on the tongue. You have only to open your heart to it.

A little girl I know visited a local animal park with her mother, and when she saw the peacocks in full feather she stopped dead in her tracks. Her eyes grew enormous and she whispered, "Look, Mommy, look! Their chickens are in blossom!" Even at the zoo— beauty remains!

Music

The beauty of music is a source of deep spiritual nourishment. Aldous Huxley said, "After silence, that which comes nearest to expressing the inexpressible is music."

Harmony is not created by everyone singing the same note. Harmony is many different notes from differing voices, all blending and enhancing one another—interconnected, interdependent. Life, too, is made harmonious by the blending of many voices. Beauty is born of the blending of many notes.

Beauty and the sacred

Our spiritual center or soul is the place of *awe*, wherein we are set afire by the sparks of beauty and power in the universe. It is the home of courage, conscience, kindness, forgiveness and thanks-giving. It is the residence of delight, of laughter, of sympathy, of beauty and of love.

When we speak of beauty as a spiritual value, we are speaking of a nearly universal good. Beauty is one of the great principals of Native American spirituality. The Dinee of the Navajo spoke of walking the beauty way, and what that meant was walking in harmony with the beauty of the natural world.

The songs of the Southwest Indians expressed their identification with the crops they planted and the animals they hunted, and gave them voices. When people identified with these natural beings, they could not treat them casually, but had to deal with them personally. They became aware that these creations had rights—at the very least the right to respect and appreciation.

Native Americans looked for the beauty and care in the world around them and then gave thanks for it. They sang to their crops in their own voices and in the voices of the plants, and showed respect for the animals as their kith and kin. They found delight and beauty everywhere. A Navajo *hogan* (house) song ends each line with the words "delightful house." The word delightful (*hozho*) also carries the connotation of beautiful. To the Navajo, nature is simply beautiful, peaceful, full of religious meaning and worthy of communion and praise.

Another culture that venerates that kind of beauty— holds it in high honor, respect, and reverence—is the Japanese culture, where beauty is expressed in simplicity. To the Japanese gardener, in the Japanese home, or in creating a Japanese flower arrangement, less is more. Elegance and simplicity stand tall. This serene reminder of the holy touches our minds and hearts as we gaze upon simplicity. And beauty remains.

POETRY . . . energy,
    in metered economies of words.
    True poets practice brevity, restraint;
    Forgoing self-important adjectives,
    Excessive ego, flowery flourishes.
    The wise have learned simplicity alone
    Ennobles truth, gives meaning clarity,
    Lets beauty be not wasted or ignored.

Beauty is its own excuse.

The venerable philosopher and wordsmith Ralph Waldo Emerson in writing of beauty may have inspired John Greenleaf Whittier. In 1847 Emerson wrote:

If eyes were made for seeing
Then Beauty is its own excuse for being.

Two years later Whittier wrote:

> *Art's perfect forms no moral need*
> *And beauty is its own excuse;*
> *But for the dull and flowerless seed*
> *Some healing virtue still must plead.*

The flowers by the roadside need not feed anyone because they feed the spirit and remind us of the grandeur of creation. Aristotle tells us "God is mightiest in power, fairest in beauty, supreme in virtue...seen through his works themselves." And so we look at the works of creation—the primary most awesome of miracles, our children—and what we see is beauty. No matter what the line of brow or chin, the color or shape of eye, the texture or tone of cheek, there is beauty there because of the miracle that is another precious life. So we choose to see the beauty, and the beauty remains.

The arts enhance our humanity.

Humans are the animals who laugh and cry, who remember their history and question their death. And it is through the arts we express the memory and the quest. Art is a great source of spiritual strength, renewal, and spiritual growth. The arts—music and singing, storytelling and theatre, dance, design, graphic and fine art, any craft raised to its highest form of beauty—these are among the rare gifts of the spirit that make us human. It is through the arts we kindle and shine forth the divine spark of our humanity.

A story from the great African American preacher Howard Thurman is set in a small but exclusive antique shop in Manhattan. One day a person of questionable background entered the shop and asked if he might look around. He was clean enough, but shabby and clearly not a potential customer in this high-ticket establishment. The owner, however, nodded and granted permission to the man to look around. He gazed at the beautiful furniture, bric-a-brac, and artifacts long and carefully. He stayed for nearly an hour. Then he left.

A month or so later the man returned and once more studied the beautiful objects in the shop, and a month after that, came back again. Finally he chose an exquisite glass piece and handed it to the shop keeper, asking if he might put it aside and pay it off week by week. It was very expensive. The shopkeeper agreed to the arrangement and the man came in weekly to pay money toward the purchase of his *objet d'art*. When it was paid for, the shopkeeper wrapped it gently and handed it to his customer. Having seen the man so many times, over so long a while, he felt comfortable to ask, "Tell me, friend, what will you do with that glass piece?"

The man smiled and said, "I have a very small room across town, with just a bed and a desk and several beautiful things which I have managed to buy over the years. I put them there because, you see, that is where I live."

Our treasures, our things of beauty, are always "where we live," and we will live—give our hearts and our energies and our hard earned pennies where our treasures are. I wish for you an abundance of beauty and the eyes to see the treasures and choreographies of the cosmos.

Inner beauty

A dear lady who is in her silver years, and quite lovely was talking with me about her habit of carefully, artfully putting herself together when leaving her home for any reason. This is something I truly appreciate and admire in everyone, and especially in someone who has been ill, or is aged, or has special challenges. Mrs. Jay, the woman in this story, told me about wearing her "navy blue with the epaulets," and how everyone she met on her way from a visit to her grandchildren had been so enthusiastic, telling her, "You look wonderful!"

You look wonderful—not just your clothes, although the effect had indeed been chic and handsome. It was something else they saw in addition to the well-styled curls and the graceful lines of the suit. It was the passion for life, the joy and excitement the lady radiated. It was the kindness that glowed from her face, the peacefulness of her inner light, and the gratitude she freely expressed for the blessings of her life. It was beauty of spirit, the beauty of love.

Caring for one's person, creating a pleasant picture for those around us by good grooming, aesthetics, careful choice of colors and fabrics seems to me a kind of salute to the beauty of the universe. When I see someone who has taken that extra bit of care in putting himself or herself together, I often compliment them and thank them for brightening my day. It pleases me to see my sisters and brothers celebrating life and their own dignity and worth and gifting those they meet with thoughtful care of their appearance.

The dark part of concern with appearances is the vanity that pays more for a showy car than I paid for my first house. It is the ostentation that misdirects the world's resources into building huge mansions when the streets are filled with homeless mothers and their children. Among the deadly sins, that can be considered a sub-section of avarice. Vanity is not in your hairstyle, but in your value structure.

The beauty of roots and wings...

It is said the greatest gifts we give to our children are roots and wings. We give them their beginnings, their foundations, and we send them forth into the vastness of the sky. The wings are inspiration, freedom, growth and possibility. And here is the paradox (I'm just full of those!) Often it is our roots that provide us with wings. Our history grounds us, but it inspires us also. Books—which represented for my children the rootedness of their home and safety, their very beginnings, also provided the wings of discovery, self-expression, creativity, and fantasy.

Looking at personal roots, mine are in New Jersey and New England. When I came to California in 1975, I looked for a place to raise my girls, my two youngest. Son, Mark, was already in college at Dennison University in Ohio, and June, the eldest was settled in Maine. I looked until I found a *Leave It To Beaver* street in Fullerton, where the girls would have good schools, safety and a hometown neighborhood.

We are molded by the places of our childhood. There are some of us who are "street smart" because we survived the city struggle. Some of us require for our very existence the sight of the almighty hills, or perhaps the open freedom of the prairie, the music of the river rapids, waterfall or surf. Think back, where are your roots?

We are rooted in beauty and love.

As I look at the rootedness of my life and the lives of my children I see places—communities and camps, fields and forests, rooms and hidey-places. I see trees, and moving water and mountains. And books. And people, neighbors and family. I remember smells and music and cuddly creatures, and secret hidden places of the heart. Mark at twelve was the Tom Sawyer of a rural Connecticut town, with his raft and his island on the creek. Kristi had a healing stream where she went for comfort, and as a child, I had a brook where I found arrowheads left for me by the Lenni Lenape.

Trees

Appropriately enough, the strongest root symbol for me is to be found in trees! The silver beech beside the house where I grew up, the wild cherry that held my swing, and the oak that bore the hammock. The laurel bush that became a little make-believe house for a tiny girl, and the weeping mulberry that hid us in its cool center. The high branches where I climbed to sit and read. I remember visiting Texas as a young woman and grieving for the tall trees of home. In Vista, California, the Palomar Fellowship raised a generation of children and gave them their religious education beneath *the worship tree*. And one of them even grew up to be married beneath those sacred boughs. Do the stars perhaps symbolize roots for those living in places without great trees?

Fragrance

How like the womb are many places of the heart, where we are rooted—the playhouse, the barn loft, the tent or camp-out porch, the closet in the breakfast nook where a tiny girl-child plays at nesting. My daughter Kristi tells me her roots include smells, and for those of us who are olfactory, this seems natural. Mark, blindfolded at camp to explore and briefly share with the blind the experience of sightlessness, knew his mother by her scent of strawberries and cocoanut. Perhaps the nose gives us wings as well, for we are told the swiftest path to the emotion's memory is by way of odors. I am taken back to Germany by a certain windy essence, to puberty and my early sexuality by the fragrance of alfalfa. And I fly away happily on the smell of summer rain, autumn leaves, campfires, or my sister's favorite cologne.

There are people who represent our roots—family, neighbors, teachers—and they too, like books, are givers of both roots and wings. Values root us. Yet they also set us on our way and enable us to fly. Noble beliefs can give us wings.

Songs and stories

Music gives both roots and wings. I loved to listen to music when I carried my children, and pre-birth experiences must surely be rooted. I like to recall that Kristi first moved within me at the Academy of Music, in response to the magnificent Philadelphia Orchestra led by Eugene Ormandy. And Amy responded to music winged with dance from the time she could move. Theatre gives us the beautiful wings of imagination, as do films, books, and works of art.

Going places in the car as a family, all snug and safe together, gave both roots and wings. Like the homesick snail, we carried home along with us, sang songs, played word games and laughed a lot. Of course we didn't dare go past a bookstore without going in, or Mark would puddle up and weep. Taking your home along sometimes meant taking your own pillow, a baby blanket, or Pooh Bear and Lovable Furry Old Grover. Sometimes it means taking a journal to write in.

Rooted and sent aloft by words of wisdom

In my ministry, I am both rooted and sent flying by our foreparents in the faith. Saint Ralph (my fond nickname for Emerson) in his divinity school address provided both roots and wings for me when he said, (pronouns changed with apology) "The true preacher can be known by this, she deals out to the people her life—life passed through the fire of thought." Emerson also tells us that one who is aware of his or her own higher self or inner beauty is inspired to share this gift with others, and indeed impelled to do so with "solemn joy...sometimes with pencil on canvas, sometimes with chisel on stone; sometimes in towers and aisles of granite; sometimes in anthems of indefinite music; but clearest and most permanent in words." And so I am a poet. Winged with words, God's spy, charged with speaking the ordinary with extraordinary precision and clarity. The truth I knew and didn't know I knew until I gave it form upon the page, melody and texture on the tongue.

Givers of roots and wings

Wings and roots affirm us in doing and being. Who and what sent you on your way? When I was a child, a neighbor who had only boys welcomed daily visits from this little girl, and became a kind of confectionery aunt—Aunt Floss. She took me to the symphony, and to see *Fantasia*. She met me "at the Eagle" in John Wanamaker's department store, Philadelphia, and empowered me to venture out into the world alone. She trusted me to make Jello in her kitchen and gave me wings of culinary freedom. My Papa gave me winged feet to dance, and the mystical airy freedom of oneness with water, teaching me to swim, as I later learned to sail. I tell you all this so that you, too, will recognize the roots and wings of beauty in your life and offer them to those you love, and even to strangers you meet.

Who gave you a glimpse of your own beauty? A friend, or lover? a poet? a child who looks like you? Who recognized your gifts? Affirmed you? Honored you? Who said "You can do it!" Who trusted you and believed in you? These givers of roots and wings are bringers of beauty and we are thankful for them, every one! Move now, beyond gratitude into heartfelt appreciation of all things bright and beautiful. Create beauty. Surround yourself with it. Share it and be glad.

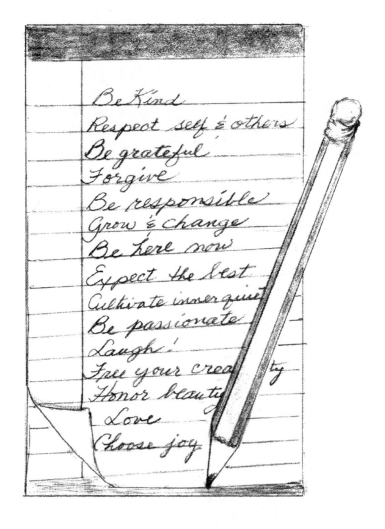

. . .a plan to improve your life

CHAPTER TWELVE

Creativity Creek

Free your creativity.

One Writer's Solution

Self-medicating some call it
dosing oneself for pain with drugs or drink
but I have learned my way to do the same
when stress or emptiness have made me think
I need a crutch or cushion to survive
and know no chemical can do the trick
how to remember joy being alive
without regret with mind and spirit quick
I turn instead to keyboard or to pen
and write
and write
and write
and yet again
I find the comfort that a writer finds
when singing dancing speaking truth in lines
of verse or metered prose or simple phrase
and for the gift of words the muse I praise

You, too, are creative.

Whenever I ask a group of people who among them is creative, the response is laughingly sparse. Few of us ever recognize our own creativity. But I ask again, a different question. Who of you has ever used something for a purpose other than the one for which it was intended? How about you. Have you put your pens and pencils in a coffee mug, your keys and change in a candy dish, perhaps? Have you rearranged the living room furniture, wrapped a pretty package, added a flourish to a note, a scarf to your ensemble.? Have you adopted a plan to improve your life? Have you dared to entertain children? If the answer is yes to all or any of these, you are creative.

Have you ever been called a dreamer or a *visionary* in that sneering tone of disapproval? The beginnings of creativity are in dreaming or daydreaming, yet all too often people will disparage the dreamers. The scientific reality is this: the subconscious and the super-conscious speak in the language of pictures—visions, imagery, dreams, daydreams, and insights. Visualization is the beginning of *creation*. To be a visionary is to see with the mind's eye the possibilities, the potentialities, the plans and blueprints of what might be. To be a dreamer is to be both prophetic and creative.

Rearrange it, upend it, make it new.

Through the years one of my most treasured toys was an old- fashioned simple kaleidoscope. This is a tube lined with mirrors through which we can gaze at just about anything, and discover a unique new kind of beauty. It demonstrates for me the heart and soul of creativity. In this type of kaleidoscope the viewing window is clear glass, empty rather than housing pieces of colored plastic. It takes a little slice of the real world and rearranges it into a new design. This is exactly what you must do in creative mode. Take a piece of your environment and look at it through the mirrors of your own creativity. Rearrange it, upend it, make it new.

Making the spot where I'm planted more lovely through the years, I have enjoyed freeing my own ordinary day-to-day kind of creativity. To provide a partners' desk for my co-minister and myself, I bought metal file cabinets, painted them brown and faced one each way, front to back, then topped them with an eight-foot wood laminate desktop. When the partner left, I simply reversed one file cabinet and turned the desk into an oversized one-person extravaganza.

In the attic of the old parsonage in Connecticut I found a red drop-leaf kitchen table which, when stripped, turned out to be solid oak. The legs were long and the table's leaves short, so it was an awkward gangly-legged misfit until I decided to cut the legs to coffee table length, and it's beauty and versatility shone through. Trust your eyes and your aesthetic instincts and discover new ways to enhance your surroundings.

Through the years, my sister gave me a collection of Strawbridge and Clothier's Philadelphia-themed three-dimensional Christmas ornaments made of ultra thin gold-hued metal. There were images of Broad Street with Mummers marching and the William Penn-topped city hall, Betsey Ross House, sculling on the Schuylkill River, and two New Jersey lighthouses. They were lovely, but so slight they seemed to disappear when hung on the Christmas tree. Eventually, I grew tired of hiding them away after the holiday, and decided to showcase them instead. I glued each one to a navy blue velvet-covered cardboard and placed them in gold frames to create a beautiful Philadelphia wall décor.

Creativity can show up anywhere. Some people are creative in the way they name their companion animals. A lady in the next town took her dog to the groomer and when asked the dog's name, she answered, "Shameless." The startled groomer asked where that name had come from, and the lady said, "I got the idea from my brother-in-law. His dog is called Brazen." What the groomer had yet to learn was the family's last name—Hussy.

The power of story

This journey of ours in search of serenity has spawned many stories in homage to rabbinic wisdom. The great rabbis have always known that storytelling is a primary vehicle for teaching and finding our way. We humans live in story as fish live in water, and Jonathan Gottschall wrote: "We are, as a species, addicted to story. Even when the body goes to sleep, the mind stays up all night, telling itself stories."

Stories come alive as we enter into them. If you simply tell me something I will probably forget. Show me and I'm likely to remember. Involve me, and I will surely carry it with me into my life. Stories bring with them energy, tears and laughter, and as we recognize ourselves and our own lives in the tales, we become involved.

In my life, authority and wisdom are expressed in poems rather than polemics, stories rather than statutes, discoveries rather than decrees. And when I write, my deepest understandings sometimes refuse to reveal themselves in ordinary prose. They demand melody, rhythm, meter, and power. My best thoughts strive to be shortened, condensed, and transmuted into poetry in metered economies of words. I sometimes believe my thoughts actually generate themselves in iambic pentameter.

Is there perhaps a song in the ether waiting to join with me in writing a poem? The "collaboration" happens as I open myself to the cosmos and allow the words to simply flow from pen or keyboard. The saying of an inner truth comes through me, not from me. The writings are often a surprise to me when I read them.

The muse at work—or not.

One morning long ago I made a trip to the beach with my merry clan, and a sea mist covered the sun. When we arrived at the shore I lay on the sand and pondered—explored and questioned some of life's absurdities and wonders. I thought of ideas I wanted to record, to capture in literary form, but I was so relaxed and comfortable, face down on my beach blanket I did not stir. Eventually, as lesser thoughts paraded through my mind, I mustered enough energy to break away from meditation and write. I reached for my tablet and ballpoint pen and waited for those deep and worthy thoughts to bespeak themselves. There was only silence—the empty corridors of my mind echoing with the laughter of a mischievous Muse.

> *Oh, wispy misty muse who guides my pen,*
> *You light a spark, a candle now and then.*
> *You spin a thought in colors I can use*
> *To weave a pattern bright. But when you choose*
> *You play a game of teasing hide and seek*
> *You tiptoe through my mind, give me a peek*
> *At some idea, some image I must write,*
> *But when I reach for paper, you take flight.*

Clearly, I thought, I must learn to rouse myself when the Muse calls. Years went by, and poems grew into books. And once again came the call to create...

Return of the Prodigal Muse

> *It's the middle of the night*
> *When everything is dark and still*
> *Or would be, were the town less light*
> *In the middle of the night.*

In the middle of the night
My mind gets busy, makes me dizzy
With the things that I must write
Though it's the middle of the night.

In the middle of the night
Thoughts force me to leave my bed
And stare at the computer light
That almost blinds me, it's so bright.

In the middle of the night
My wicked Muse inspires a poem
Belatedly and just for spite
'Cause it's the middle of the night.

Your life story

In a life and career management seminar the bright, dynamic speaker announced to her audience, "Your life story is a lie—something you made up—and you can change it." Now, isn't that enough to curl your hair? How do you change your life story? Stop and think about it a minute. Our life stories are, like everything we say, only an approximation of reality. The Taoists tell us that the Tao that can be put into words is not the Tao. Yahweh told Moses "I am that which is." The divine, is beyond human language. So when the seminar leader says "Your history is something you made up," it's a dramatic way to make you look at your responsibility as co-creator of your life's reality.

"Who is in charge of your life?" You have chosen your present experience, and although you have unlimited choice you are never free of the consequences and effects of your choices. In those circumstances which are beyond your control (I choose not to be short of stature) you choose how you will act and feel and be as one of the short people or as whatever your life circumstances have named you.

Be careful what you assume.

You manage or create your future by what you intend to do and what you assume is possible or likely to happen. Your goals, your intentions and assumptions are all-important because they actually transform your possibilities into realities. In those cases where your goals and assumptions disagree, the assumptions will prevail. We live our "as if's" in agreement with our unconscious assumptions, so this makes it very important to clarify for yourself what those assumptions might be.

Someone once proposed a ninth Beatitude: "Blessed are they who know what they are doing, for they shall know when they have done it." Not too different from the statement in *Alice In Wonderland*: "...if you don't know where you're going, any road will get you there." Unless you're clear about your beliefs, your intentions, assumptions, direction and purpose, you won't know if you're off course. Direction and purpose are vital elements in your life journey. Check your map, or the GPS.

As you free your creativity, you will also require objective education and information to keep on track, and education happens only when we are ready for it. A teacher cannot give you knowledge, only data and the inspiration to listen to the truths you may have known and not yet recognized.

Correct the course, but don't quit.

It is less important to be talented than to be committed. Don't give up. Lazy talent produces nothing, while the commitment expressed in persistence opens doors to achievement. It may be necessary to re-evaluate, regroup, and plan new strategies when something is not working. However, making an honest evaluation and renegotiating goals is far different from giving up in anger, disaffection, or defeat. A trustworthy person can be depended upon to fulfill an agreement, not to quit.

Sharing

Once you have allowed yourself the thrill of recognizing your creativity, you will find deep satisfaction in sharing. To ask a creative favor from someone is in fact to give them something precious. Being invited to use our gifts is highly rewarding.

for mark, amy and kristi
who allow me to help
from time to time

put me to work
give me a task
I can be useful
if you but ask.
I'll lead a retreat
or I'll write or design
and help you by using
these small gifts of mine.
being part of new projects
both major and small
enlivens my spirit
when there is a call
for my help or my guidance
my thoughts, words, or art
all so ready for sharing
your trust warms my heart

The gift of the cracked pot

Creativity is not about perfection or flawlessness; it's about making use of even our brokenness. A Zen teaching story features a cracked pot. Crafted to carry water, one of a pair of water pots grows old and develops a crack in its side. Because of this damage, the pot leaks half its contents every time it is used to bring water from the river. This might be a wasteful process, causing only loss of time, effort and resources, but the wise carrier made use of his creative thinking and the pot's imperfection. He planted flower seeds along the side of the road where the spilled water would fall, and created beauty using the pot's precious flaws. All of us are sometimes like the cracked pot, and our flaws, too, can bring beauty to the world.

Meditation Over Ham and Eggs

Why here? Alone…
in some small restaurant
does sweet
creative thought
enlighten me?

Surrounded as I am
with teeming life.
the whirr of conversations,
laughter's tune…
I yet find quiet
at the very heart of me.

Why here— while cradled
In the noisy quiet,
enveloped in the crowded solitude,
does some strange joyous magic free my mind
and send the grace notes
tumbling down the page?

I sit content,
alone and not alone
awaiting inspiration…and it comes!
I learn new truth and speak it note by note
connected and at peace
I touch the Source.

Open your mind to new possibilities, rearrange the
ordinary, look with new eyes, and become quietly
creative

. . .it's a performance!

CHAPTER THIRTEEN

Laughter Light

Laugh! Be outrageous.

This is the way I have lived and chosen my path…
creating a household filled with laughter and
sunshine for the children and other growing things.
There are those who have called this foolish.

If I were not a fool…
  I would long ago have recognized defeat
  And given up.
If I were not a fool…
  I would stop laughing in the face
  Of poverty and disappointment,
  And start thinking life is a drag.
If I were not a fool…
  I would refuse to love.
  I would stop seeing stars in the grass,
  And rainbows in an oil slick…
  And stop singing about beauty
  And life's minor miracles.

If I were not a fool...
    I would stop believing in magic
    And in myself.
    I would stop flying kites,
    Chasing hot air balloons
    And dancing my shoes off.
If I were not a fool...
    I would grow up,
    And grow old,
    And become occupied
    With matters of consequence.
I would be practical and businesslike,
    And matronly...
    And forget about living with music
    And merriment
    And a white hyacinth.
If...
    I were NOT a fool.

If it will be funny in a year, it's funny now!

One of the most powerful of inner resources creating personal wellbeing and peace of mind is laughter. Humor is the gift that will enable you to bear the unbearable and do the impossible. Laughter is the music of the soul. It can make you well and keep you sane. This is among our more rare and precious legacies. We must be able to laugh at life's funny side, to recognize a vast sense of humor at work in the universe, and refuse to take ourselves too seriously.

As I tell young couples who come to be married, the things that go haywire and threaten to ruin their big day will make a great story for years to come. And remember—if it will be funny in a year, it's funny now! Look at the funny side. And if it isn't fun, we may not be doing it right.

Smile.

The softer side of laughter is the smile, a simple lifting of the facial muscles that brings with it comfort, pleasure and a feeling of safety for the recipient. Anger, with its frowns, is a secondary emotion, fear gone underground. You need to meet your fears, honor them and let them go. With fear as the darkroom where we develop our negatives, the struggle to bring in the light and create a positive outlook requires that you exchange fear for love. You can choose. When you are upset, ill, or downright angry, scowls, pained expressions, and stern looks carry a message of dislike and even threat to the observer. Smile! Please make the effort, and smile; or if smiling through is beyond your capabilities, cultivate a pleasant neutral look. A smile is easy on your face and reflects on the faces of others.

Take a minute now to frown. Really make it a good one.

- Scowl!
- Can you look disgusted? (No laughing or smiling allowed.)
- Disappointed?
- Distrustful?
- Dismayed?

Good! Now, smile. I don't care what thoughts were going through your head, smile anyway! It takes a lot less energy and effort—actually fewer muscles than the frowns required. And you know what? That smile is creeping down into your body, clear down to your toes. It's invading your attitude. When we smile it affects our endorphins, and we can't help ourselves—the smile begins to erase bad feelings.

Laugh!

Laughter is even better! Who can see someone laughing wholeheartedly and not be moved to join in? And just think of how Norman Cousins prolonged his own life by watching old comedies and administering the miracle drug of laughter.

William Shakespeare said, "A merry heart goes all the way; a sad one tires in a mile." You can choose a merry heart. Give yourself permission to laugh, be daring and even a little outrageous. To be outstanding takes courage, but the rewards are immense, life affirming, and delightful.

Live fully and with zest! My sister June knew how to do this. She loved purple, or more specifically she loved lavender and violet. She even drove a lavender car, although the manufacturer's official color name projected a more sophisticated tone and hid the truth of the car's purpleness. When June was forced to fight the demon cancer she, like all those undergoing invasive chemotherapy treatments, lost her beautiful silver hair. Fortunately she had access to good natural looking wigs, and maintained her normal external beauty wearing a coif styled just for her. One day her son, knowing his mother's sense of humor, brought her a fluffy violet clown wig, knowing she would laugh. June laughed. And then she did the outrageous. She put on a purple dress, plopped the pastel wig upon her head and went to chemo therapy, spreading the laughter and her own brand of sunshine to all her fellow sufferers.

Choose to be happy.

You don't have to earn joy; it is a gift of grace. It is written in *The Jerusalem Talmud*, tractate Kiddushin, chapter 14, paragraph 12: *Persons will be called to account on judgment day, for every permissible thing that they might have enjoyed . . . but did not.*

When my four children were preteens, teens, and young adults still living at home they gloried in riotous competitions to see who could best embarrass Mom. When out together in the car with mother behind the wheel, the family frequently became so raucous Mom had to pull off the road and stop, blinded by tears of laughter. Laughter ruled and outrageousness was the norm. The family punch line was, "I'm crazy, not stupid!" taken from an oft-told favorite story. Around the dinner table a bit of wackiness, funny faces, or an outrageous scenario was quite acceptable and even treasured, whereas outright stupidity would never be. Funny stuff lives up to its root word "fun."

I'm reminded of a community service that was to be held at the local Roman Catholic Church, in which three Protestant ministers had been invited to participate. One was to lead the singing, one to read the gospel, and one to present the sermon. The priest robed up and went into the narthex with the acolytes to prepare for the service, and as he looked up and saw the three other clergy entering the sanctuary he realized there were no chairs placed for them. He whispered to a lay leader who was seated nearby, "Please, Robert, three chairs for the Protestants." The old gentleman didn't hear him, so he made his request again, a little louder, and this time Robert heard—or thought he heard—something. He rose slowly from his pew, shaking his head doubtfully, and turned to the congregation. "This is highly irregular," he said, "but I have just been asked to lead three cheers for the Protestants."

And for all of us. Three cheers! We are one. The beloved folk poet, Rick Masten, taught us to let life be a dance—through the bad times as well as the good, whether leading or following, in sunshine or rain, joy or sorrow. "Share the laughter," he wrote, "bare the pain" (let it show), "without the dark there can be no light." Life is a dance, and the motion—the eternal dance of the cosmos—urges us to action, inspires us to do something joyful with our lives, to follow our bliss.

There is a popular proverb that goes like this: "Life isn't about waiting for the storm to pass, it's about learning to dance in the rain.

To Dance in the Rain

'Twould be so easy to give up on life
To rant and rage against the dark,
And yet there is a gentle side to life
That whispers hope... and lights a spark.

The fire ignited warms the soul of me.
The image in my mind is clear...
A campfire with the family gathered round,
And friends, with laughter shared and tears.

Life's tragedies bring lessons learned,
Not always welcomed, rarely sought.
Yet in the eyes of loved ones shines
The tender gift the "dark" has brought.

Our common journey, on a stormy path
Each hoping to transcend life's pain,
Will need a dream, an inner truth,
That sets us dancing in the rain.

Consider the dandelion.

Some time ago I came across a story about an elementary school teacher who had a special lesson to share. It was springtime, and she told her class about something she had seen on her way to school, and asked if they might have seen it too. "I saw it coming up from the ground," she told them, "about ten inches high, and on top of it was a little round ball of fluff, and if you went woooof, a whole galaxy of stars flew out." She asked them, "What do you think it was like, before the little ball of stars appeared?"

One little girl said it was a bright yellow flower, like a sunflower, only very small. "And before that?" the teacher asked. Someone said they saw it as a tiny green umbrella, half closed, with its yellow lining showing. And even before that it was a little rosette of green leaves coming out of the ground. So, what was it?

The children thought they knew. "It's a dandelion!" they shouted. "Well, yes, she said, "and no. If you were to pick what you're calling a dandelion, it might be one of the things we've just mentioned, but it could become the other things, and it's so much more. You can't capture a dandelion. It's really a performance!" And so is every living thing—a performance! You are too, like the dandelion, a performance!

Named for the lion's tooth, and golden-maned as the sun, the dandelion is the most maligned of flowers. The very strength and independence we might admire in this glorious survivor is an excuse for anger and frustration if we choose to name her "pest" and "weed."

For those who love her, however, the hearty dooryard dandelion is a shining sunburst, her buds a quaint umbrella, her leaves a tasty salad or an herbal tea; she is the source of a delicate country wine, and brightens our landscapes and our imaginations. And what child can resist delight in the flight of her silver seeded parachutes at the puff of his lips?

This flower—the dooryard dandelion, nourishing and strong, cheery and free, with character enough to inspire the passions of both enemy and friend—I have chosen as my personal totem or symbol, my logo (from *logos*—the word, sacred symbol for the wordsmith and poet.) I let it stand for family, strength, and beauty, near my safe and welcoming door.

Orange monkeys

Ray Bradbury, prodigious writer and poet, was a kind and friendly man, who willingly came to speak at local bookstores and churches. When a beloved colleague introduced me to him at our favorite meeting place, Books Etc., I spent the afternoon in conversation with my new friend and writers' role model. I told him about my son, away at college at that time, regularly and generously writing letters to his mom... letters that made me laugh with their whimsical humor, letters that showcased Mark's writing talent and his quirky mind. Bradbury said, "Mark is an orange monkey, like me. I, too, was an early writer, whimsical and quirky...different from the others, an orange monkey."

You needn't aspire to be an orange monkey but you certainly shouldn't hide the bright fur of your humor, your quirks and foibles, your willingness to be unique in all the world. Now is the time to celebrate your childlike and mischievous side. Wear that feathered hat, that whimsical tee shirt. Send a funny greeting card. Embarrass the kids just a little. Laugh out loud and let yourself be outrageous.

Be Mine

. . . the sweet or funny messages of love

CHAPTER FOURTEEN

Love Lake

Love is being with...

If love is the answer, could you please repeat the question?

Lily Tomlin

Love is the answer...
to all questions.
It is the form love takes
that must differ.
Love feeds the hungry,
soothes the hurting,
warms the chilled.
Love challenges,
encourages, inspires.
Love celebrates and grieves.
Love mends.

Love teaches and learns,
acknowledges,
and admires.
Love answers.

George Eliot said, "I like not only to be loved, but to be told that I am loved; the realm of silence is large enough beyond the grave." How do we speak our love? We speak *with* persons beloved, not to them or worse, at them. We connect.

Learn to *be with*... If you are truly with someone or something you will be fully present, centered on that special creature or event without distraction or competition. Let the people beside you feel they are truly important in your world. This is the hallmark of love. Be completely with your favorite music, your animal companions, your garden. Be with people in acceptance and support. Be with your body in activity and rest. We are an interconnected web. There is no us and them, there is only oneness.

Valentines

At the heart of the month of February (pun intended) are the lace and ribbons, the flowers and candy, the sweet or funny messages of love. Valentine's Day—a restless holiday it is, dancing to the rhythms of love songs and sighs. It is the time we've set aside for telling long-time friends and lovers, families and new-found pals those special words of affection or thanks left unsaid most of the year. It is the time when I rejoice in remembering my mother's singular gift to me of the true spirit of hospitality—teaching me to expand my heart-room that there might always be house-room. And I remember Papa's gifts of smiles and dancing feet. In years past it was the time when I sent hugs thru the ether to my sister and my friends across the country.

It is the time to think of the many gifts of love we all receive. Love makes lovers beautiful, philosophers gentle, artists alive to the world of wonders about them. It opens our eyes to miracles and our hearts to both joy and pain. Love's changes perpetuate themselves in beauty. Here is a visual and verbal Valentine in the shape of a basket of flowers—

VALENTINE

Intensity....integrity...intimacy
listening...learning...reaching...teaching
centering...searching
finding...touching
in touch and
touching
connecting
coming home.

When I moved to the west coast from New England, Valentine's Day in California felt devastating to me and to anyone *uncoupled*. We criticize excessive commercialism at Christmas, but the advertising in the second week of February was every bit as overwhelming as any holiday ads throughout the year. Aimed at sweethearts, mates, romantic and connubial pairs, it made the lone individual painfully aware of his or her single status.

In contrast to the gold hearts and red roses approach to the holiday, the engineer of a little ride-upon mini-train at Travel Town in Griffith Park delivered a short spiel before each circuit of his tiny train. He urged both adults and children to remember their special people on Valentines Day—brothers and sisters, grandmas and grandpas, hubby, wife, mom, dad. "And you don't have to spend a lot of money," he said. "Just a flower or a handmade card, a little note that says, 'You are so special and I love you very much.'"

Now that is the spirit of Saint Valentine—the poet imprisoned and alone, who remembered all his beloved friends and sent them beautiful messages. I imagine the notes written in calligraphy by his own hand and signed "Your Valentine." He was saying I am yours. I am with you in my heart, even when I cannot be with you face to face. To embody love is to connect and build bridges. The bridge builders help us to see our oneness. Like the great Maya Angelou they teach us "we are more alike than we are unalike."

Building bridges

Whenever I think of bridge builders, I recall the story of a lovely dream. A gathering of theologians, with their great minds and deep ponderings, had hewn great blocks of concept, hypothesis, system, and belief with which they built a complex and elegant tower on the far side of a rushing river. The ordinary, extraordinary people gathered near their homes on the other side. Quietly they gazed at the high structure in wonder and amazement. They could neither reach the tower nor understand what it might mean.

Then the wise men and women among the people spoke together, wept together and lamented— "Had the theologians only chosen to build a bridge across the river rather than their ivy tower," they said, "we might have met in the middle of the river and discovered love." This is love in its larger meaning—building bridges whereon we might meet our brothers and sisters and know love.

It is most interesting, how we human creatures respond to one another. We are more likely to be lonely when we are in the same space with a disaffected other than when we are alone, yet we can be truly with one another across miles and beyond touch if we so choose. To be beside someone when they are not truly *with* you creates an ultimate loneliness.

Love story

JD, the grandchild whom you met in the forgiveness chapter, is now in his twenty-first year, and we have been lovingly *with* each other in every one of the twenty-one. I just discovered, among my notes, this love story about Justin at age two.

1995 - I wear glasses in order to see clearly. A certain little boy, however, (my grandson) hates my glasses. To him they are not something to help with seeing or connecting; they are barriers between us. So—every so often he attacks them, yanks them off my nose and flings them across the room—a behavior I strongly discourage, considering the cost of frame and lens. But when that beautiful little person grabs my glasses from my face and immediately and vigorously rubs noses with me, I'm hard put to scold or correct him. Somehow my vision is improved by the removal of my glasses, as my heart is touched and we are connected—*with* one another.

Ruled by love or fear

People live their lives from one of two basic positions, sometimes slipping in and out of both. The two positions are fear and love. When you perceive someone as attacking you, either you are operating from a position of fear, or that person is. We don't attack unless we feel threatened and think by attacking we can demonstrate our strength at the expense of another's vulnerability. You won't misinterpret another's good intentions as an attack unless you're functioning from fear. Anger is a secondary emotion born of fear.

Now here is a truth that some will find frightening— you can choose your own experience of reality. If that statement makes you angry or defensive, remember that the only basis for anger is fear. When I say you create your own reality, I recognize that you can't change the external world or other people. You can, however, choose how you perceive and experience the world, yourself, and others.

You can choose to replace fear with love. What we experience is our assumptions, our inner state of mind and belief system projected outward on a screen we call life. What we see out there is really a mirror image of what we harbor in ourselves, our own thoughts and fantasies.

Fear produces only movies of war and conflict, even when they are disguised as our romantic ideals. Ask yourself:

- Do I choose to experience peace of mind or conflict?
- Do I choose to be a love finder or a faultfinder?
- Do I choose to be a love giver or a needy love seeker?
- And when I am in the midst of my interpersonal transactions are my verbal and non-verbal communications loving toward the other person?
- Are they loving (as they need to be!) toward myself?

Transparency

Many years ago, when I was co-minister to the Unitarian congregation in Bangor, Maine, a friend gave me a gift of love and transparency. He called me over to a table where we were displaying Values posters I'd selected to decorate our sanctuary, hoping they would pay for themselves when some of them were sold to members and guests. This man, by the way, was introverted, practical, and rational—a successful engineering professor. He pointed out one of the posters and said to me, "Here's a topic for a sermon."

The poster read, *"Our lives are shaped by those who love us; by those who refuse to love us."*

"We can get 'cookbook' instructions about sex," my friend said (Remember Alex Comfort's book, *The Joy of Sex*, a takeoff on Irma Rombauer's *Joy of Cooking*?) "but nobody tells us how to give and receive love... tell us that!"

"Friend," I thought, "you just did it. You gave me love in a big way by trusting me with such a topic, by trusting me with your self, and being vulnerable enough for those few brief moments to share with me a true concern." How shall I meet this trust? Why, by giving myself in return, by being with this friend lovingly. Which is to say by sharing my authentic self with him.

The Transparent Self, by Sidney Jourard was for me a treasury, a wellspring of ideas to plumb, in which I recognized my own life. In it Jourard said that love and trust would spawn and indeed require self-disclosure—something he called transparency. Strive to know the person you love and permit her to know you, and thus to love you.

We make ourselves vulnerable if we disclose ourselves. Even in families we often hide behind roles, relating to my husband or my mother rather than relating to the persons themselves. The question, "Who are you?" can too easily be answered by one's role—wife, brother, teacher, activist or physician. Your self, however, is your subjective side—what you think, feel, and believe, what you want or worry about. That's the part of you that's dynamic and growing, the part that makes it possible to relate, to love.

Roles are static and rigid, like a porcelain shell hiding us from human sight or human touch. Perhaps we hide because we're ashamed and afraid due to the impossible images we carry of what we ought to be. We awfulize and "should" on ourselves. Part of this comes from stereotypes—the tools of little minds incapable of fathoming the complexity of human individuals. Yet everyone is unique and special in just being a self!

You are far too precious to hide.

I knew a young woman in Bangor who created problems for herself and others by telling lies. She wasn't malicious or even truly immoral. She was simply unreal—creating a dramatic, brightly colored plastic self to boggle the eyes and minds of those she met. "They wouldn't be interested in me if I told them the truth," she said, "I'm so dull." Friends, no authentic, growing human being is dull. You may not share interests or even vocabulary with a particular individual, but everyone is interesting and valuable to someone—just as she or he is!

Exercise in Self-discovery

Who are you?
Who are you, you ask...
And yet a deeper who
Are you?
I am poet, nurturant woman, playful child,
Softly scented body, silken skinned.
Medley of meanings, feelings, needs...
Sensuous and vibrant, loving life.
I am these, and ever more than these.
Who am I, I must ask...
And who am I?
I am my dreams, I am my hopes, my fears,
A self who reaches out to touch and know,
A person who is willing to be known...
>*Trusting...*
>>*Even now...*
>*Trusting.*
Scent of strawberries and cocoanut
Sunlit silvered waves and upturned mouth
I am sparkling eyes and warm embrace.
I am understanding.
What do you pretend?
That I am not afraid.
How can we be close?
By sharing.

I once had, in my dining room window, a small, simulated stained- glass window, given me by a loving friend. It was adorned with this brief verse by William Blake: *I looked for my soul and my soul I could not see;/ I looked for my God and my God eluded me;/ I looked for a friend and then I found all three.*

There is a search going on in the lives of each of us, a search for the elusive self; a search for the spiritual center of our individual reality or the soul; and a search for meaning in life, for the ultimate, that power which undergirds life and make us whole and integrated—*the sacred.* This is manifest in ideals, words and action, in the gifts of wonder and grace, and it comes to fruition in loving relationship.

To cherish another's wellbeing...

Love is expressed in the living of *Shalom* which is caring that things improve for the other person, wanting him or her to be successful, assuring your friend that it's OK to live well while doing good. Love is expressed in challenging the loved one, inspiring, urging, advocating, respecting! Sometimes the loving thing is to stop rescuing someone or managing her life, to stop smothering or absorbing him. And sometimes it's even wrapped up in saying goodbye.

Love makes us strong.

Once, in another life, as a business and communications consultant and desktop publisher, I did more than create beautiful words and graphics; I built teams and taught success techniques. It was my challenge to "grow leaders." Successful leaders are people with personal strength, people with that special something we call *character*. When developing a technique for creating this kind of leadership some years ago, I began by asking myself the question, "What makes us strong?" and one answer immediately sprang into my head from an inner knowing—love! Love makes us strong.

The image of the 120-pound mother lifting a car off her child's leg comes to mind with dramatic impact, but strength is not limited to feats of muscle power. There is strength in overcoming fears of all kinds, strength in facing a challenge, strength in every act of kindness or courage. It is not willpower or a sense of duty that gets a parent up in the middle of the night to feed or comfort a baby—it is love.

At the time I was exploring these ideas, *love* seemed like an unusual starting place for building success in the business world. I could just imagine the reaction in corporate America to a book or speaker advocating the building of business and professional success through l-o-v-e. Then one day I found support for my theory on an early morning television show.

During an interview on "Good Morning, America," in April of 1988, Jan Carlzon, the CEO of the highly successful Swedish Airline, SAS, cited love as the source of power which opened new methods of commercial growth for his corporation. Host Charles Gibson pointed out that the Swedish government sector provides more than half the jobs in the country (63% of GNP) He then said to Carlzon:"...*you've got a tremendously large government sector, the government providing so many jobs, tremendous job security in this country. You really can't fire people. That being the case, how do you get—how do you motivate the workers?"*

Carlzon's response was my affirmation. He said, *"I think in all respects in life people are motivated by two factors, love or fear.* (Doesn't that sound familiar?) *And love in the way of a company stands for respect and faith in people. I think that the security system we have in labor in this country shows an attitude in the society where we feel respect and faith in people and by having this situation I think that people dare to take risks. They're not afraid to make decisions because they could lose their job the day after. I find very much in the United States that you manage people by fear, and you shrink the capacity of people so that they don't perform to the limit of their capability..."*

Love, in this context, is clearly not an emotion, but a way of being and doing in the world. It is relationship in action, it is teamwork, it is friendship, it is first and foremost, respect. We see the results of Carlzon's respect in the trust he places on ordinary workers in SAS, putting the decision-making power in their hands to create good service. Respect equals love, and respect is expressed in action.

Relationships teach us, support us, enable us. The product of our shared energies far surpasses the sum of our individual efforts. With our loved ones and friends, our co-workers and neighbors, we create synergy—the whole that is more than the sum of its parts. Each of us is a model and an inspiration to those around us, and each can act as mentor and guide to someone else who might be at a different place on the path than we. All this is demonstrated repeatedly in those organizations where warmth and humanity are salient characteristics. The strength of any organization is directly related to the *loving quality* of its people.

Being there for someone

What do you say to a friend who is in pain, on the brink of despair, or has suffered a great loss? Do you really need to say something wise or profound or enlightening? Do you have to *do* something?

Unfortunately this is a particularly difficult question for the men in our society. Men feel the need to act on any unsettling or problematic information they receive. If you tell a man about a problem he believes he has to fix it! Men are problem solvers. Women, they tell us, are the sharers of feelings. A woman will usually require and give a sympathetic ear—a hearing of a person's troubles, with appropriate expressions of solidarity or emotional support. This difference in response may cause communication difficulties for mixed gender sharing. But wise counselors have advocated an acceptance of one another's feelings that includes all of us.

Love is being with...If I care about you I am likely to say I'll be there for you, and then I will be there! That doesn't mean I'll pay the loan you default on or weed

your garden because you hate to see it overgrown—
although I might do that too—but it means I am
consciously with you, paying attention, valuing you
and affirming you. We need one another, whether
in times of crisis or simply in day-to-day living. We
recognize our existential solitariness, and we yearn
to be touched by the lives, the shared humanity of
others. The loving connection, the being with, requires
you to listen, to be in touch with the other person, to
simply BE, and to give the gift of total attention.

It's the love you put into the doing.

Some years ago, on public television, I saw a
documentary made for a United Nations anniversary
celebration, which told the heartwarming story of
Mother Theresa. The most effective and moving
aspect of the film for me showed Mother Theresa's
gentle touch. As throngs surrounded her, as she
greeted her nuns or the poor, the sick and hungry
in their beds, her work-worn hands reached out to
simply touch. A benediction and a healing seemed
to rest in those noble hands.

Mother Theresa said, "It is not how much you do,
but how much love you put into the doing." She
assured us that everyone has a vocation to bring
love to those who hunger and thirst for it, whether
it be amid the depths of poverty, or in the shelter of
our richly comfortable homes. Not many are called
to vows of poverty or works of humble labor among
the sick and helpless, yet each and every one of life's
children can be a messenger of divine love.

An old poster suggests, "Bloom Where You're Planted." Somehow, that message takes on new meaning in the light of the words of Mother Theresa and these from Saint Francis of Assisi:

That where there is hatred,
we may bring love,
where there is wrong
we may bring forgiveness,
where there is discord
we may bring harmony...

Being with is sharing. It is sharing others' excitement or sadness, their joys and concerns; sharing meals, stories, worries, laughter and tears. It is checking on your roommate with the flu, and bringing a cup of tea, a piece of toast. It is mingling.

MINGLING

For every human personality is at last
a mystery and a secret...locked away
from every other living soul
by the failure of language
to bridge our isolation
and unlock the oneness of the cosmos.
Tiny windows of the spirit
open to one another as we peer thru
translucent metaphors
which only dimly begin to reveal
the commonalty of the human experience.

So...

Mingle with mine your laughter,
and we will be a bell choir
of merriment and joy...
pealing out new harmonies—
shared chuckles, giggles,
chortles and guffaws...
nourishing each other
with the zest of our delight.
Yet never fear to mix your tears with mine;
the salty contrast of shared sorrow serves
as accent to the honey of our smiles.

Listen, learn, and love.

The late Professor Leo Buscaglia often spoke of his deep concern for our failures of communication and their effect on love. "We just don't listen adequately," he said, citing the example of the waitress who, when we order black coffee, asks, "With sugar and cream?"

Buscaglia, known as Dr. Love, grieved that elders attending his presentations so often would cling to him and confide that they had not been hugged or touched in years—possibly since a mate died. "What's wrong with us," he lamented "that we let these beautiful people die of touch starvation."

Some time before his final illness Buscaglia had a cardiac episode, which put him in the hospital. He hated being held prisoner by the dehumanizing little cotton gown flapping open behind, and being spoken of as the *cardiac case in 214*. "How dare they!" he would shout. But with love in his heart he overcame the impersonal, inhuman aspects of the experience.

Being the public figure he was, the beloved Dr. B. was gifted with multitudes of flowers, cards, and magazines, as well as people to visit and be with him. His concern, however, was for the dear old soul down the hall, admitted on Medicare, staring at the ceiling all day long in a darkened room amid strangers, without anyone to visit her or help her to heal herself.

He truly cared, and so he limped down the halls of the hospital, one hand behind him to keep his posterior covered and the other hand filled with flowers to share. His face was a pale sun wreathed in loving smiles, and his great spirit reached out to everyone who was lonely, hurting, and afraid. He visited with the elderly lady and then with others. He was *with* these new friends, and he brought healing to them as he healed himself by loving them.

Changed by giving love

Vincent Van Gogh said, "There is as much difference in a person before and after he is in love as there is in an unlighted lamp and one that is burning. The lamp was there and it was a good lamp, but now it is shedding light too, and that is its real function."

In this little gem, Van Gogh uses the expression "in love," but I would like to borrow the wisdom from Vincent and share it with this small change:

There is as much difference in a person before and after he gives love as there is in an unlighted lamp and one that is burning. I believe this description, this metaphor of the lighted lamp, pertains to all loving connection. It is not limited to what we think of as being in love.

We are changed by giving love—our real function. You give light by being with another and articulating your shared humanness, your solidarity with your fellows.

Words of love

How do you speak your love? Do you enter true dialogue with interest in the other persons, being one hundred percent present for them? Communication meets deeper needs than the passing of information. It is the ground of meeting and the foundation of community. Words have both cognitive and affective meaning, they convey both information and emotion.

Love grows fresh and new as you speak another's name in love. Take time today to surprise a loved one with a phone call, a note or some little gift—just because. That's what we do when we are willing to be with...

. . . a heap more in the cutting and sewing than there is
in the calico

CHAPTER FIFTEEN

Joy City

Choose Joy.

We have forgotten what once we knew:
"We are one with the cosmos."

We yearn to touch, to connect,
To reawaken our knowing
And re-member
our dismembered Oneness.

"Therefore it is in Oneness that God is found and
they who would find God must themselves become
One..." Meister Eckhart (12th Cent mystic)

Yes, in joy you shall go forth,
In peace you shall be brought back.
The mountains and the hills before you
Shall break into song,
And all the trees of the countryside
shall clap their hands.
        Isaiah 55:12

You have a choice.

Shannon, a young wife and mother, has been through repeated upheaval over the past few years. Her beloved husband suffered a devastating catastrophic illness. She has juggled trips to the hospital, hours at her darling's bedside, comforting the family through the loss of their grandmother, trying to pay bills when the money wasn't there, and struggling to keep life normal for three active children. Still she maintains her faith, her sweetness, and her smile. Shannon confided in her best friend that she just hates to hear people say, "I don't know how you do it." She quips, "I didn't know I had a choice."

We always have a choice—not about life's hurtles, but about how we meet the challenges. Greatness is our birthright, yet most of us walk through life unaware of our potential. We must step beyond the daily chaos and become all that we can be. Shannon didn't choose her husband's illness, or material, emotional, and physical trauma. These were thrust upon her. She chose, however, to meet the challenges with courage, kindness, and a positive spirit. And she kept strong her faith, and her ties with family and friends. Shannon chose transcendent joy.

We see things not as they are but as we are.

John Murray wrote that when he became convinced that all of humankind are in harmony with and a part of the Divine (Universalism) he regarded his friends with increasing affection. We need one another, whether in times of crisis or simply in day-to-day living. We recognize our existential solitariness, and we yearn to be touched by the lives, the shared humanity of another. We create our lives as we experience them, and wise voices through the ages have urged us to create beauty, peace and love for ourselves. "Turn the lemons into lemonade," they say, "see the glass as half full, not half empty." But remember the secret truth of that message: we see things not as they are, but as we are!"

My own metaphor for these universal truths uses those unpopular plants that inhabit every garden, path, and roadside meadow, the flora most of us call *weeds*. When you look at the tangle of green and gold that is a field of wild mustard, do you see weeds? Or wildflowers! It is your choice.

It is your divine gift and responsibility to make choices—every minute of every day for the rest of your life. You choose. You can choose to live life, or to sit on the sidelines and whine. You can choose to see the funny side, or to weep.

When I say "Choose joy!" I'm not denying the sorrow, grief and tragedy in the world, nor am I talking about mere pleasure, nor even happiness.

- *Pleasure* I define in sensual terms—
  that which feels good, tastes good,
  smells good, and gives delight.

- *Happiness*, I define as the customary
  human response to life's gifts—the good stuff.

- *Joy,* however, transcends.
Joy goes beyond happiness
as a spiritual response to life itself,
even in it's darker manifestations.

Adela Rogers St. Johns puts it this way, "Joy seems to me a step beyond happiness. . . a light that fills you with hope and faith and love."

A longitudinal study of the sources of joy found overwhelmingly that relationships are what brought joy. According to Harvard psychiatrist George Vaillant, "Joy is connection."

To age like fine wine

Aging is a word that conjures up visions of gray-haired folk struggling with walkers or dozing in rocking chairs. But have you ever stopped to consider that every one of us is aging from the day we are born? Aging is a life-long process, and *Coming Of Age In America,* a book title I seem to remember, doesn't quite say it. Do we ever really come of age?

I think that book was about something called growing up, but growing up doesn't happen once and for always. It is a recurring miracle and a mystery. It is a threat and an inspiration. And it requires of us an incredible amount of flexibility and humor to survive the relentless passage of the years and the ever-escalating speed of change—and to do it with grace and dignity.

The goal is to make the days and years work for you in your spiritual and emotional development—to age like fine wine. This demands a special attitude, a present-living, forward-looking attitude that will not allow you to solidify, to crust over, mire down, or atrophy. You need an attitude of wide-eyed wonder even in the face of harsh realities.

Dealing with change through the years

Once upon a time... Do you remember this? Little boys and girls were taught that they could make life-shaping decisions at age 5 or 10 or 18 or 22 and determine forever and ever the paths their lives would take. You can be, in these United States, (they were told) just about anything you want to be—if you believe in God and work hard enough. That was the boys, of course. For the girls, there was the opportunity to marry success by the same magic formula, with a pinch of good looks and sex appeal thrown in.

When Sam—your great-granddad, perhaps— decided at 12 to raise his own calf and learn to be a good farmer like his daddy, he had a fair chance of inheriting the farm and doing just that over a lifetime somewhat shorter and infinitely less diverse than his children and grandchildren could expect. His career choice was made once and forever. When he stopped being whatever that little boy or young man had decided he would be, he retired, and that was that.

Or was it? We now know our career decisions are not forever, but there are many decisions about the way you live your life, the way you will age and mature and ripen, that you make all along the way, all through the years.

There is no doubt that every one of the life-changing, character forming decisions made by the high school senior, the young bank clerk, the bride or young mother I once was, has effected the overall pattern and direction of my life. Each has played its part in bringing me to the place I am today. That's the way it is with all of us. Which is why the wonderful Robert Frost poem, "The Road Not Taken," provides such a powerful image for most of us. "I took the one less traveled by, and that has made all the difference."

Evolve

You can't retrace your steps or go back, months or years or decades later to the places you were—whenever. But you can make new decisions that will take you to the someplace you'd prefer to be tomorrow. You can evolve into the future rather than just slithering out of the past.

Choosing...
Every minute each of us is choosing,
Selecting what we'll do and be and say.
Life's co-creators, each on our own pathway
Yet One in the human journey day by day.
Choosing.
Chosen...

Shamen, leaders, mates and priests are chosen
By gift, by love, by calling, or by lot...
To love us—share a life empowered, enriching
That we may live aware of the joy we've got
We've Chosen.
Choose joy!
Spirit of Life is this sweet Joy transcending—
Rising above all sorrow, fear or pain.
Expressed in kindness, breathed in gentle teachings
Like grace, our birthright, gifting us again.
Choose joy!

What will you do with your forever?

Life isn't always easy. We are constantly being
bombarded with problems—world problems, social
problems, money problems, business problems, and
interpersonal problems. It's enough to make a person
a little cranky, if not downright ugly. There are, in
fact, times when it feels like your little boat (planet
earth, the U.S. economy, that precious commodity
called peace, or maybe your Toyota Corolla) is about
to flounder in the midst of a stress-making storm
of cosmic proportions. So how do you ride out the
storm, and reach your destination? How do you
avoid drowning yourself in existential despair?

Clearly, you must first have a destination or goal,
a sense of *mission*. By mission, I mean more than
immediate goals, I'm talking about what you will
do with your forever, the map to that which gives
meaning to your life.

These are questions most frequently left unasked by educators and parents, and yet the *journey* is at the heart of every worldwide myth and teaching story. "Mission" is what Joseph Campbell called *vision quest*, a dedicated journey in search of the ultimate good you can see only in your heart, or with your mind's eye.

A few summers ago, (quite a few, according to my calendar) I was being interviewed on an early morning inspirational television program, and the host asked how we can tap our inner resources for personal power and strength. I said clarity of mission was vital to personal power.

"Write a mission statement," I said. When the host asked how I went about writing my mission statement, I told him that as a writer, I simply wrote it down. Oh, boy, what a cop-out! That was neither an accurate answer nor a complete one. Belatedly the process became clear.

The keeping of journals and writing of my thoughts has always been very much a part of both my spiritual and professional life, but as I pondered the process of creating valuable insightful documents, I recalled some triggering mechanisms I'd used to discover my mission for myself. The motivation for writing my mission statement first came from a book on getting organized in which the author demanded that, before turning the next page, the reader must write a life mission statement.

I'd helped to write the mission statement for a camp and conference center, and for my own congregation, so why not? First I noted:

- what I wanted to broadcast with my life,
- how I hoped to relate to others,
- what I hoped to accomplish, enjoy and discover. And finally
- how I wished to behave in the world.

I later molded these deeply personal notes into a poem that would join the others in my first book. This was the result:

in this life it is my prayer to articulate and share
a message of love, of peace, of choice...
and to sing the "divine perhaps."
to be to my children until the end
wise teacher, playmate, trusted friend;
to live joyously, kindly, fully, well,
knowing grace is the gift of laughter;
to continue with zest as long as I live
to learn, to discover, to grow, to give,
to behave with respect toward all that is,
and be worthy of its returning.

Had I been more acute during that TV interview, I might have given instructions like these I offer you:

Think for a moment about your mission.

- What do you want said of you when you die?

- What "gifts" do you most want to give to the world?
- What makes you happy?
- How do you intend to live your life? Honestly? Lovingly? Intelligently? Courageously? What are your particular adverbs?

Decide to be happy.

Henry David Thoreau said, "From the right point of view, every storm and every drop in it is a rainbow." And this also is true...through the veil of unhappiness every hill looks like a mountain. You can turn the predictions of experts and the lessons of the past into rules and limitations, or you can choose to be a dreamer who brings your dreams to life.

The decision to be happy is actually a decision to stop being unhappy. You can live consciously, root your actions in clear intention and celebrate the miracle of who you are. You can choose love over hate, peace over conflict, and happiness over wretchedness. In making these choices you seed and nurture the human landscape with distinctly tender and joyful hands. Decisions for happiness become decisions to make every day count.

Joy

A quotation from Ellen Willis in my *Woman's Journal* said, "My deepest impulses are optimistic, an attitude that seems to me as spiritually necessary and proper as it is intellectually suspect,"

This somewhat cynical quotation inspired a response
I called

Above Suspicion.

Where optimism may be
intellectually suspect,
Joy is above suspicion
and honored by the wise
of all the ages.
Joy is the zest for Life
which rises above
tragedy and despair
to celebrate the salt of tears,
the honey of delight.

And when I read in the same journal that Rosalind
Russell said "Taking joy in life is a woman's best
cosmetic," I was quick to respond... *and a man's*
greatest strength.

I believe in you.

I believe in you...just as I must believe in myself. I
treasure even yet the myth of human goodness—so
fragile, yet so much stronger than that old puritan
image of depravity bolstered by guilt and fear. There
is a delicate, yet flexible and unbreakable dignity
to my myth. Because people care, because we are
willing to struggle to improve, to go the distance,
because the human spirit refuses to quit or to regret
"what we did for love"...we will prevail!

I certainly recognize that we are not in charge of the circumstances that assail us—illness, catastrophe, war, or the loss of a loved one. But each of us is in charge of our own life. You are in charge of the way you respond to all life's circumstances, the way you choose to perceive life and yourself. I bid you in happiness or in the presence of the deepest sorrow, to give thanks for the good and look for the gift. You will find berries of nourishment even among life's thickest brambles, when you choose joy.

Welcome to Joy City!

AFTERTHOUGHTS

Particularly telling are the things I have chosen to leave unsaid, the places I've decided not to go on this tour of the State of Serenity. I had no inclination to speak of diet and exercise, nor of prayer, or hard work.

With responsibility, passion and creativity, the part of success usually attributed to hard work is covered—without the stress. And prayer is quietly tucked away amidst gratitude and generosity, in tranquility, mindfulness, choice and love.

Diet and exercise is all too well explained and exploited everywhere else by everybody else, and an upbeat serene attitude is more likely to heal than to require healing.

I keep running into behaviors that need to be sorted out, sometimes my own. Some afterthoughts are quite demanding, which is to say they absolutely had to be included in the body of the manuscript. Late night wisdom *a-Mused* me, inspiring further commentary. (That mischievous Muse at work again.) These thoughts I then necessarily included, although I had previously believed the chapters were already complete.

And not all of my latent ideas appeared in the dead of night. I noted in the grocery store that I should remind my readers to be more aware and do a better job of being kind than the fellow in line ahead of me.

Later the word "doom" loomed across my monitor and I knew I had to inveigh against catastrophic (gloom and doom) messages, the kind posted even by the "good guys" in hopes of scaring more money out of their members and friends. Arrgghh!

ACKNOWLEDGEMENTS

A huge thank you to Jim Walker, the creator of Jimmy'z Imagez, for the beautiful artistry of the front cover photograph, "Montana Road to Rainbow Mountain."

Thanks to Mark Somers and Kristi Kawas for helping the writer to strengthen her literary voice, clarify and crystalize meanings and sing out when she might have whispered. You are loved and treasured.

Love and appreciation to Carla Picogna for listening to the author's other voice (the spoken word) through 15 chapters of Serenity and to Amy Budds for listening-in to the last third of the book and smiling her encouragement.

Huge grins of gratitude and love to Gail Marshall for voraciously devouring the printed pages—"More! send me more!"

Thanks to Dr. Jerry Metz, the Rev. Jon Dobrer and the Rev. Meg Riley for inspiration. "Carry the flame!"

And waggy-tail, lickey-face to Toto, Monkey, and Stevie dogs for their unconditional love and companionship.